4695

EX, ORIN,   AGI

D0489384

Journeys into the Art of C

EXPLORING DRESSAGE TECHNIQUE

Journeys into the Art of Classical Riding

PAUL BELASIK

J.A. ALLEN · LONDON

First published in Great Britain by
J.A. Allen & Co. Ltd
1 Lower Grosvenor Place
London sw1w 0el

1994

British Library Cataloguing in Publication Data
A catalogue record for this title is available from the British Library.

ISBN 0-85131-606-9

Line drawings by Dawn Caronne, Dianne Breeze (chapter openings)
and Maggie Raynor (Chapter 6)

Typeset by Textype Typesetters, Cambridge
Printed and bound by Dah Hua Printing Co. Ltd, Hong Kong

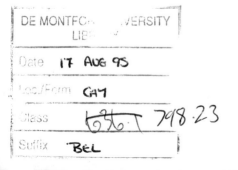

Contents

Acknowledgements

I WOULD FIRST LIKE to thank my wife Jeanne, for her countless hours of help in editing and preparing my manuscripts.

I would also like to thank Caroline Burt at J.A. Allen, for literally years of guidance; also Lesley Gowers, who has worked with me over every word of this book and *Riding Towards the Light*. A special thanks to both of them for their initial faith in me when these works surely seemed uncoventional.

I thank Dawn Carrone for her illustrations, which to me are works of art; also Maggie Raynor and Dianne Breeze for their artistic contributions.

To Paul Saunders for his cover designs.

I'd like to thank Lorell Jolliffe, my assistant, for help in the research on lateral work.

Finally, thanks go to the University of Pennsylvania, in particular the library staff at New Bolton Center, for allowing me to read and study from their great collection.

Paul Belasik
January, 1994

Prologue

LET A MAN DECIDE upon his favourite animal and make a study of it – let him learn to understand its sounds and motions. The animals want to communicate with man, but *Wakan Tanka* does not intend they shall do so directly – a man must do the greater part in securing an understanding.

Brave Buffalo, Standing Rock
(Frances Dunsmore, Teton Sioux Music,
Smithsonian Institute, Bureau of
American Ethnology Bulletin,
Washington DC, 1918)

Introduction

WHEN I HAVE TALKED to musicians and dancers who were in the middle phases of their training and practice, to see if there was one common thread, it was often a conscious and unconscious infatuation with technical bravura. It is as if the growing mastery of the human body and the growing mastery of the body of knowledge that one is immersed in, constantly needed to be tested, stretched, challenged and extended. In any art one is continually faced with historical examples of great artists' past work, as well as the work of one's peers which is in front of you at every performance, exhibition, and/or competition. Comparison is logical. When in dressage competitions several players perform the same work or test, and this piece of work is rated by a panel of judges, comparison becomes further entrenched. The eye and the mind begin to focus on the differences of the performance, but they must focus on the measurable attributes to quantify and verbalise – the height of the piaffe steps, the number of canter pirouettes, the straightness of the changes, the conscious elements. The Journeyman has to be involved in this kind of investigation to develop his riding knowledge. There must be an understanding as complete as possible of all the various exercises, movements, training systems, and there must be an ability as complete as possible to execute all the various exercises, movements and training systems. There has to be complete freedom in and a familiarity with all these techniques.

However, to stop the Journey in the land of technique can be deadly for the growth of the rider. As D.T. Suzuki[1] has suggested, very often people confuse true harmony with tranquillity. You will get all the tranquillity you need in death. To revere tranquillity is to revere death. To revere life is to revere movement, change in all its forms, lovely and frightening. If ever there was a creature of movement it is the horse, whose beauty and grace can be concealed in a stable or at rest, but is revealed in its motion. The art of riding is a celebration of motion, of nature's rhythms. A great ride cannot be preserved and sold for millions of dollars after the artist's death. It always possesses a very fair immediacy. The rider must live and work in the present, always grounded in the here and now.

All of the names of the Japanese martial arts end with the word 'do' meaning 'the way' – *Karatedo*, open hand way; *Kyudo*, the way of the bow. The way, the process, what is important, is that every individual art has a metaphorical property. Each is a reference to something more communal, more universal, namely, the process of life, or as Carl Jung might say, individuation. Master the metaphor and it may tell you about life. Get stuck in the metaphor and you could die. For the rider, getting stuck in the land of technical bravura can be the end of his advance on the journey of horsemastership. In order to get through, though, you must first go in. After the measurable techniques, there are the unconscious elements, the mythic elements, where the art of riding has always come from – where creativity lives.

What follows are some of my trips as a Journeyman in the land of technical bravura. When you travel in that country, and you return to a city where you had once been, it can be completely changed. This need not be fearful because Xenophon, the Duke of Newcastle, Pluvinel, Eisenberg, La Guérinière, Baucher, Steinbrecht and on and on, have all left some beautiful maps. Most important of all, Nature has presented riders with the horse on which to travel.

Chapter One

A Fog of Walks

'THE SCHOOL WALK of the old masters was a diagonalised walk in which the horse lifted his legs and collected himself.'[2]

Nuno Oliveira

A friend of mine who is a trainer and dressage judge had the idea of staging a symposium for upper level dressage riders, trainers and judges. The notion was to allow for some frank, constructive discussion about the current state of dressage in the United States. He had invited the trainer H.L.M. Van Schaik to present a keynote address. For my part, I was to serve in some capacity as a moderator and to interview Van Schaik as I had done many years before in a forum that I had arranged in conjunction with a large horse organisation in Pennsylvania.

We decided to make a fast two-day trip up to Van Schaik's home in Vermont, in order to cement some of the logistics and to meet face to face for discussions. It was in the middle of winter and our destination involved about an eight-hour drive in the heart of the north-east ski country. The forecast was stable, and we decided to take my friend Michael's four-wheel drive truck. With our wives covering for us we took off in the early morning. As we drove through the day we had a chance to talk about many things – our children, our families, but especially horses. Michael and I are the same age and have similar educational backgrounds. We have a mutual love of riding and an admiration for some of the same old masters. (Michael's family has been instrumental in promoting dressage in the US for a long time, and it is only because I have the utmost trust in his integrity that I agree to get involved again in the administration of large groups.)

We drove throughout the day and in the dark we made it into southern Vermont where we stopped to refuel. It was one of my first visits north for a while. To step outside the truck into the northern winter air was refreshing. I walked around the truck and looked out across the street beyond the bright glow of the station lights. It had been a relatively mild winter so far. When I talked to the station attendant he told me that the skiing was off because of insufficient snow. I could only see traces of snow in patches where it had been ploughed into piles. The bare ground was frozen deep and hard. I always feel a similar excitement and apprehension in cold weather –

some psychological hold over from the old days of living a simple life in a northern climate where the temperatures can get seriously low and make little things very difficult.

Soon we were off again for the final leg toward Cavendish where Van Schaik lived, near the top of a high hill just outside the tiny village. Cavendish is a short way from the heart of the ski country in Vermont. The houses usually have steep-pitched roofs and you can smell the wood smoke from early fall until spring. The mountains are old and numerous, and each has its accompanying valley. Many little villages line up in these tiny valleys all through this country. It can give you a remote feeling, and adds to a sense of privacy. When the great Russian author Alexander Solzhenitsyn decided to come to the United States, of all the places, he chose Cavendish. It seems it could fill the requirements for a reclusive life.

If it weren't for the skiers on holiday, on any given winter's night, the roads would be empty and everything closed. Coyotes have returned to the area, and howl in the clear night air.

As we get closer the mountains rise up around us. More and more snow is now visible and the ground is all white. Icy patches glow like phosphorus in the moonlight. Deep in the small valleys clear streams, moving too fast to freeze, spin and steam up the air with larger and larger ice bridges forming over them. Through the winter as the spray condenses and vapour freezes, fine layer upon layer is formed.

When we finally arrive at Van Schaik's, it is cold. Our legs are cramped, and we are tired, but as soon as I see the old man I feel revived. He has cooked dinner for us and greets us with drinks. We have some discussion and fun, and continue more in earnest the next day. We try to prepare the symposium, and several times Van Schaik shifts the conversation to another topic. It is clear to me after

[13]

last night that he is excited about something, the way a scientist can get excited with a new finding. I think he must be preparing to write about it. The subject that seems to have him enthralled is the diagonal walk. I am familiar with this idea through experience with Nuno Oliveira and his writings. However, I also know it can be a confusing topic. It seems that the old masters used to use this diagonal walk, as Oliveira has mentioned, as a preparation for the 'gentle passage'.[2]

When Van Schaik shows us a copy of his address, it begins: 'I have been called the "crazy old man", and some people doubt if I am mentally still all there . . .' Of course, anyone who can write a statement like that and can then deliver a lucid address with some very pointed advice and criticism, must be very sane and very aware. I listen but I have heard it many times before, and in all honesty am thinking of the interview. If this diagonal walk comes up, which is a good possibility since he seems currently enchanted by it, I can just imagine the thoughts of the competitive dressage riders in the room. When we start calling this two-time trot-like gait a walk, they *will* think he is crazy.

I know from past experience that many of these people have no interest in the ancients and only know about gaits asked for in dressage tests. We finish some more work, but before long, we have to leave. As it turned out, that was one of the last times I saw the old man alive.

Van Schaik was not crazy in calling this diagonalised movement a walk. But the diagonal walk which resembles a kind of preliminary passage, a soft passage, is hardly the end of the subject. Let us look for a moment at the idea of a trotting two-time walk.

In the sport of racing harness horses, there are races for trotters and for pacers. Pacers race in a two-beat gait, but unlike the trotter, which propels itself off diagonal (*con-*

[14]

tralateral) pairs of legs, the pacer propels itself off its *ipsilateral* pairs of legs – the legs of one side having the same stance phase and the same swing phase. The left front and left hind move as one ipsilateral pair, and then the right front and right hind move in their turn. So we have this two-beat gait which can reach racing speeds. Now, in the walk, the horse can move in a four-beat sequence: right hind, right front, left hind, left front. All dressage riders live in fear of closing up this sequence – some by pushing the walk too hard, some by holding it back too much. In any case the ipsilateral pairs move closer and closer together in timing until they have the same stance phase and the same swing phase, and the horse is pacing at the walk. So we get a gait that, in terms of one description, is the same as the racing pace. In both gaits, the horse is being propelled by its ipsilateral legs, which are paired together with a similar time in the stance phase – i.e. when they are on the ground – and a similar swing phase – i.e. when they both travel through the air. The amazing thing is that if you show even the novice rider a horse that is pacing, he will easily be able to tell when it is pacing at the walk and when it is pacing at the trot. Other factors of speed, suspension, etc., are involved in discriminating the gaits of the horse. So what do we have in the pacing walk, a two-beat gait at the walk? Not many people will disagree with that. Then what about a diagonal walk? Could that be just another two-beat gait at the walk? The diagonal walk is not necessarily as pre-posterous or illogical as it might first seem. I have already said, though, that the diagonal walk is hardly the end of the story.

There were and are many differentiations in the walk: counted walks, Spanish walks, pacing walks, ambling walks, school walks, collected walks, extended walks, running walks, etc. It is my feeling that the old masters were in no way sloppy horsemen in that their gaits seemed to be so open-ended and apparently impure. I think I can prove the opposite: that they possessed a superior awareness of the many subtleties in any gait, and delighted in the exploration of them. If the modern dressage rider reads the texts of Pluvinel, for example, he will not recognise many of the movements so often practised at that time. How many riders today have any idea of what the *demi-volte, passade, un pas un sant, nez air,* or *terre à terre* are? The easiest thing to do is to claim that today in our competitive tests, we have evolved and our gaits are more pure. Can this evolution be borne out?

Sometime later, after I had returned from our trip, I was driving in my truck. Two days during the week, I leave the farm to give a teaching clinic. On these drives, which often take several hours, I frequently listen to tape recordings. On this day I was relistening to a tape of a lecture by Dr Doug Leach, who was a noted researcher of equine locomotion. Some years before I had arranged a seminar from which this recording was taped. This was the same forum that Van Schaik had spoken at. Dr Leach is an excellent speaker and a careful scientist who is not crazy about the colloquial expressions of gait which many of us horsemen use. He has spent quite some time and effort to get horsemen to begin to use a standard language to describe the biomechanics and locomotion of the equine.

Dr Leach's voice continues. Out of this machine comes a mild Canadian accent talking about locomotion being a reflex action with some conscious motor control. He goes on to talk about the problem of defining and categorising the different types of gait. He talks about rotary gallops, transverse gallops, cross cantering, left leads and right leads, etc. Then he goes on to say, 'but in fact – surprise, surprise! – gaits do not exist.' My attention

[16]

becomes galvanised. I am travelling on a turnpike moving pretty quickly. There is road noise and traffic. I reach for the stop button. I want to be sure I have heard it right. I rewind the tape. I turn up the volume and play it again. Yes. That is exactly what he said. I play it once more. This time I let the machine run. His voice is clear.

'There is such a continuum of changes in the limb coordination patterns seen in horses (that) when you carefully analyse the locomotion of these animals, clearly there is one whole continuum of changes which these animals are capable of. It is us in our simplified way of analysing these animals, that categorise and selectively train for specific gaits. Hildebrand in California has defined over four hundred different strides, and from his work he concluded there is no such thing as stride. I think it is important to recognise this continuum of changes does exist. If you look at the gaits of a foal you will not recognise the gaits that you see because there are so many different types that these young animals can exhibit. They have not been channelled into the gaits that we ourselves rely on. Of course, we need our old terminology, canter etc., but it is important to realise (that) the horse is capable of a whole range of motion.'

My first impression is that Pluvinel and Doug Leach would probably have no trouble talking to each other. However, a lot of people involved in dressage today will be left out of the conversation.

The first chance I get, I begin a systematic review of the relatively current and important works on biomechanics and equine locomotion. I think it is a big mistake to disregard this work because it is too esoteric or impractically scientific. In some cases elaborate force plates and strain gauges have been designed and applied to moving horses to describe accurately what is happening. In others, high-speed films taken as fast as two hundred and forty frames per second, almost three times as fast as the speeds they use in human locomotion research, have been used to describe the horse's motion. Computers have been employed and excellent scientific efforts undertaken and then replicated world-wide to give us a good idea of just how our horses move. So when a statement like 'there is no such thing as stride' surfaces, and when you get a warning from the most current literature to be aware that there is a very real continuum in the changes of horse's limb patterns, and when this also coincides with the old masters' fluid use of different gait patterns, then I think there is an important lesson for the modern dressage trainer.

For the trainer who is completely absorbed in the training of dressage horses for competition with FEI or competitive rules as guidelines, there is a significant danger. These rules are not for training dressage horses. They are guidelines for competing dressage horses. The current competitive standards for the horse at the walk are extremely limited. FEI Rule, Article 403, Sec. 2 states: 'When four beats cease to be distinctly marked, even, and regular, the walk is disunited or broken.' Only the following walks are recognised in dressage competitions: collected walk, medium walk, extended walk, and free walk. The danger is that an implication can be drawn that these are the only walks that should or can exist. This premise cannot be justified or supported by the most current scientific research on gait analysis, nor can it be supported by the historical literature of the old masters.

My point is that even if the trainer is only interested in training the four competitive walks, he must develop an experience with and a knowledge of as much of the continuum of changes of the horse's limb patterns in the walk as possible – if for no other reason than to have a way to correct or train out some of the variations of gait patterns that are bound to occur.

Many dressage trainers warn of prematurely trying to collect the walk. Why? When the horse is advancing in a four-beat rhythm at the walk, it is advancing its legs in a pattern like left hind, left front, right hind, right front. The ispilateral pairs of legs (on one side) on the left go, then the ipsilateral pairs of the right, and so on and so on. As soon as the trainer recognises this careful ipsilateral progression it becomes easy to see that if the front foot on one side slows down or the hind foot on the same side speeds up, the horse will close down the interval of time between each foot's time on the ground, or the stance phase. If it gets too close, the result will be that the horse moves from a four-time ipsilateral gait to a two-time ipsi-lateral gait: two time, because the legs of the right side strike the ground simultaneously as one beat and then the legs of the left side strike the ground simultaneously as the second beat. Simply put, the horse starts pacing.

If the trainer tries to collect the walk by loading the haunches, shifting the centre of gravity backward, he will almost certainly push the walk from a four-time rhythm toward a two-time rhythm. If the ipsilateral legs close up and move as one, then the two-time rhythm will be a pace. If, on the otherhand, the contralateral legs close up and move as one, you have a trot-like gait. Since many of the old masters were more concerned with loading the haunches than they were with keeping a gait rhythmi-cally pure, then they were not bothered it seems by this shift-over. They routinely practised the diagonal walk as an exercise to deepen the haunches. 'A horse that does not go well upon his haunches can never do well in the Manège, so that our whole study is to put him upon them.'[3] (Duke of Newcastle)

The modern trainer really does the same thing when he actively collects the walk, and deliberately presses it into the two-time rhythms when using half-steps, jog trots, and soft passages all as precursors of the piaffe.

However, if the modern trainer wishes to gather the walk and hold it in a four-beat rhythm, he must be careful to shorten and raise the steps of all four legs uniformly. Any over-zealous attempt to load the haunches and raise the forehand by shifting the centre of gravity of the horse further backward will change the walk rhythm, usually by quickening the hind steps. If the trainer gathers the horse harshly with the hand, he can stiffen the horse's neck and shoulder thus restricting the forelimbs and slowing them down. This, of course, will also shorten the swing time between the front and back limbs.

There is a valid argument concerning whether it is really possible at all to collect the walk, at least the way we usually think of collection in the trot and canter. Yet, as Van Schaik has written, the FEI language describing the collected walk, trot and canter is nearly identical.

At first glance one could think that obviously the lack of a defined suspension phase in the walk clearly shows that there is not enough power or thrust generated to raise the horse's center of gravity very much up and forward. Therefore this is why we can't think of collection in the walk. Without enough thrusting power to generate a suspension phase, it's difficult to think of collection. In order to collect or extend the stride while maintaining the same tempo, one has to change the arc of the horse flight, from a more horizontal trajectory in extension to a more vertically oriented trajectory in collection. Having said this, we will see it is not at all that simple in the next chapter. Suspension alone is not the best indicator of collection or even thrusting power. Suspension can be deceptive.

So if it is not suspension, *per se*, that makes collecting the walk difficult or impossible, what is it? I believe it is the artificial categorisation that the walk remain four-beat. It is very possible to collect the walk, just as the old masters did all the time. What is impossible is to collect the walk and keep it four beat. These are mutually exclusive ideas. This is why, in my opinion, there is so much mystery and confusion. The language of the FEI concerning the collected walk needs to be changed. If one feels that the four beats are the crucial element to the walk, then the notion of collecting it has to be adjusted. If one doesn't care if the beats remain consistent and rhythmical, then the language of collection can remain.

It is my feeling as a trainer of horses that the four-beat imposition in the walk is important. I feel there are other gaits which are better suited to demonstrate collection. I feel that the modern walk, especially the way it punctuates dressage tests, is not there so much to show range of motion within that gait, as much as it is in the test to see if the horse is relaxed. For that purpose it is a good barometer. Horses will not walk in a quiet sustained rhythm if they are too tense or if they move too fast.

'The horse cannot maintain this ordinary walk above a maximum speed . . . If the stance time were to decrease to less than the swing time, there would have to be a portion of the stride during which there would be no supporting legs under the hind end, and another where there would be no support for the front. Since the walk has no suspension phase, as do the faster gaits, it would be impossible for the stance time to go below the swing time, i.e. the horse would fall down.'

Strategically placed (and it is very important that it is strategically placed, or like a bad fence on a jumping course it can be a trap instead of a challenge), the walk is a safeguard against wreckless excitement in dressage exhibitions.

I think it is very important when Doug Leach makes the following statement:

'There is such a continuum of changes in limb coordination patterns seen in horses (that) when you carefully analyse the locomotion of these animals clearly there is a whole continuum of changes which these animals are capable of. It is us in our simplified way of analysing these animals that categorise and selectively train for specific gaits.'

A walk, then, is not 'broken' when it moves out of four-beat rhythm any more than it is fixed when it is in that rhythm. When a trainer gets more comfortable in this fog-like continuum of the walk, he need not live with a fear of breaking anything just because it changes. The Journeyman must in fact learn to deliberately evoke change, especially when presented with problematic horses. As a trainer you cannot live your life defending the philosophical territory you may have inherited. These same walls of standardisation which offer you protection can also imprison you. I believe this is a very important perspective, philosophically and pragmatically. In one system you use change – you try to stay open and fluid. In the other system you are always reducing, trying to stop change. This system of training has an inherent flaw built into it because you cannot stop nature. The trainer needs to have the broadest range of experience possible. This will open the rider's feel to more nuance. If you can ride a horse into a pace, you must be able to ride out of it. In many ways, it is a matter of perception.

'We don't teach our students enough of the intellectual content of experiments, their novelty and their capacity for opening new fields . . . My own view is that you take these things personally. You do an experiment because your own philosophy makes you want to know the result. It's too hard, and life is too short, to spend your time doing something because someone else has said it is important. You must feel the thing yourself.'

Isidor I. Rabi
Nobel Prize winner in physics [5]

Chapter Two

The Hovering Trot

'A CONVULSIVELY TIGHTENED, tense back produces artificially exalted and exaggerated steps (also called a floating trot or the extended passage) whenever the rate is increased. Similarly a diminution of the rate that is forcibly achieved by the reins produces hovering . . . Horses that display a preference for shortened gaits commit this fault very readily, especially when their tight back facilitates these hovering steps.'

Waldemar Seunig [6]

The Hovering Trot

I did not want Seunig to be wrong. His famous book *Horsemanship* was always a great map to me when I was lost. Everytime I look at it I think how it must have been received when it first came out, before a lot of the new science of biomechanics and equine locomotion. It must have been intimidating. Even today its encyclopaedic scope will humble any equestrian expert.

I have trained quite a few horses over the years, but I have only run into three horses that really exhibited this particular flaw of hovering in the trot, which at first glance resembles the horse in passage. In reality the movement is more like some illegitimate relative of the passage. It is a lofty trot which seems to go up in the air more than it moves forward. Unlike the passage, which is a great display of elastic power, the hover trot seems to dwell aimlessly. Once it is engrained it can be difficult to eradicate.

The first horse wasn't with me long enough to really work on it. The second was never really completely corrected, although he did make good progress. I decided to try to loosen this horse's back with a series of medium-trot-to-collected-trot transitions and trot-walk transitions – basically a steady diet of longitudinal flexing and extending exercises. I thought these accordian-type exercises would help make the horse's back more flexible, and then hopefully the hovering would disappear. It could easily be argued that these are the wrong exercises, nevertheless to a certain extent the hovering did disappear, but I never fully understood why. It was in trying to train the third hovering horse that I learned a lot about the biomechanics of the horse. This eventually led me to some real break-throughs in some problems with the passage, and some finer points of technique.

The third horse had been trained to passage prematurely, obviously because it displayed a tendency towards exaggerated steps. This horse was a disaster when I tried longitudinal transitions. The elevation and stiffening got worse. In downward transitions the horse's hind end bounced up and down like an empty wagon on a rough road. This inability to dampen any concussion behind was a catalyst that sent me back to equine locomotion research.

But before we can talk about corrections it is very important to know just how the horse moves in an efficient forward stride. It has been found that the horse's central nervous system triggers very precise limb movements, and there is considerable similarity in the repeating strides.[7] As the horse's hind limb is protracted (see Fig. 1a), the hoof moves forward toward the horse's centre of gravity, and the croup flexes.[8] As it impacts with the ground (Fig. 1b), there is a vertical force generated, a sort of ricochet which has a braking effect on the horse's smooth forward momentum. The planting of the hoof signals the beginning of the stance phase, which can be divided into two parts: the first, in which there is a braking effect which continues until the horse's hips are more

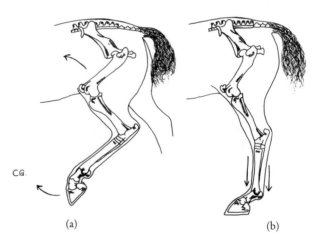

(a) (b)

Fig. 1 (a) and (b) Hind limb sequence.

or less vertical over the foot; then the second, where propulsion takes over as the horse's centre of gravity is falling or moving forward.[9]

As the hoof impacts, the powerful longissimus dorsi and epaxial muscles of the back contract to resist or to stop the upward push, or one can think of the ground trying to push the horse up into the air.[10] At the same time that the hoof impacts, the stifle and hock are flexing to dampen this shock-wave.

During the stance phase (Fig. 1 c-d), the horse's body is continually moving forward its croup and hips over the hoof planted on the ground, with the fetlock serving as a kind of hub to the spoke-like advance of the leg. Because the stifle is flexing with the croup, sort of pushing down, the femur can come forward, towards vertical, without sending the croup up against the force of gravity. This is a very important phenomenon for the dressage trainer.

Once the horse's hips pass over a vertical line from the planted hoof, the second part of the stance phase, namely the phase of propulsion, begins. The hock will be the

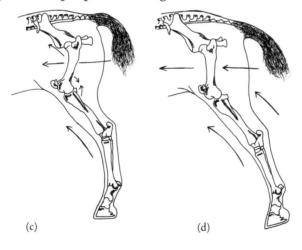

(c)　　　　　　　　　　(d)

Fig. 1 (c) and (d) Hind limb sequence (continued).

main source of propulsion. Yet even as the hock is extending, the stifle may still be flexing. This insures that the horse's weight will still be falling forward. In this way, the stifle helps the hock minimise the vertical lifting of the hips, and maximises the horizontal push of the hips. The horse cleverly sneaks around the effect of gravity, and provides a stride that is most efficient in forward thrust. As the hock extends, the superficial flexor tendon loosens and this frees the pastern. It strongly rotates forward and now propulsion forces reach maximum.

To a certain extent, although the front limbs are designed more for support than propulsion, a similar action is taking place. As the front hoof impacts with the ground, the joint of the scapula and humerus flexes and the fetlock sinks. This allows the braking forces to be absorbed and the weight of the horse to fall forward. As the front leg approaches vertical, the braking forces subside and the second part of the stance phase, the propulsion, ensues. High-speed films show the entire leg moving steadily forward,

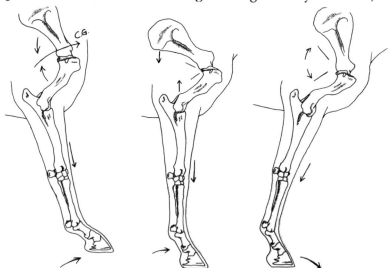

Fig. 2 Front limb sequence.

advancing spokes of an imaginary wheel which has the fetlock as the hub.[11] (See Fig. 2.)

I was continuing my review of some of the equine loco-motion and biomechanics literature when one night in the library, I came across a paragraph in a particular study that seized my attention, and in a second crystallised the whole essence of the hover trot. In this study by Kingsbury, Quaddus, Rooney and Geary,[12] they were doing some measuring using live horses and their limbs and cadavered limbs, and some differences were observed. The para-graph that explained these differences reads:

> 'The major discrepancies between live and severed limbs are to be found in the first segment of the normal, tan-gential and moment curve. The discrepancies occur as irregular wave forms and are thought to be the result of the absence of the smoothing and pre-stiffening effect of muscle on the stay apparatus . . . the testing system then provides not only positive data in the dynamics of the passive stay apparatus but also on the effects of muscle action on the stay apparatus.'

The paragraph is discussing the muscular effect on the tendo-ligamentus systems. This is what got me. The busi-ness of protracting the limbs, and then the rotation around the fetlocks with their sinking and rising, is pri-marily a reflexive action dependent mostly on tendons and ligaments. The dampening and smoothing of the for-ward impulse is muscular and largely dependent on flex-ion in the hip, stifle and hock in the rear, and the shoulder in the front.

My experiences were not jibbing with Seunig's theory. For one thing, none of my hovering horses had a particu-larly tight back, at least to begin with. In fact, two were long in the back and flexible. The other interesting matter was that all three horses were lazy in their way of going and manner. Now things were beginning to fall into place. It was the absence of muscular effort in dampening the stride that let these horses lazily bound along off their tendons and ligaments with little effort toward deepening the step or its complementary powerful propulsion.

Seunig was correct when he said that a tight back facilitates the hovering steps, but was not correct in saying 'a convulsively tightened, tense back produces artificially exalted and exaggerated steps.' My disagreement with the master is not really nit-picking or semantics, because to me there is a serious underlying principle here that is very important in trying to correct trotting flaws in many horses. It has to do with the limbs, not the back. And, later, it is crucial to understanding the passage.

One of the most magical aspects of the biomechanics of a horse in motion is how the stifle can continue to flex in both the braking stage and the propulsion stage of the stance phase – all this in order to keep the horse's hips down and falling forward, away from the force of gravity. When they work together, one extending and one collapsing, the hips stay low and move forward, thus facilitating optimum horizontal thrust. Aside from the rotation of the fetlock, which is primarily a reflexive action and therefore an action which the horseman can only slightly effect, it is really only the stifle, hock and shoulders where conscious muscle manipulation can occur. These are the areas that account for the smooth and impulsive transportation of the horse forward, or, on the other hand, these are the same areas that will collect it.

In that third hovering horse I had in training, it was precisely a lack of muscular effort in flexing the stifle and shoulder that produced the vertical bounding of the hover trot. In the stance phase up front, the knee is locked, so all dampening and changing has to occur in the joint of the scapula and humerus. Likewise, in the stance phase in the rear leg, the hock, until it extends, is fairly locked and braced, so all the dampening and changing has to occur in the stifle and hip. When the horse fails to flex the joints in the stifle, the superficial flexor tendon in the rear leg can't loosen when the hock extends and the fetlock raises against the tightened tendon. The result is that the hips are bounced upward. When this is repeated step after step the horse's centre of gravity bounces up and down with a much diminished forward impulse. What you get is hovering.

My disagreement with Seunig is that the action of the back in a broad way is a reaction to the production of motion by the legs. The action of the back is secondary to the action of the legs. Power must first be generated before the back can react to it. The action of the back cannot produce any steps at all, elastic or 'exalted and exaggerated'. The action of the legs, and more specifically the muscular action of the shoulder, stifle and hock, must produce swift, strong, forward impulsive movement. The inaction of the legs, and again more specifically the muscular inaction of the shoulder, stifle and hock, produces hovering steps. This subject is much more pertinent to the passage, which comes up later, but I don't want to minimise the importance of the back.

Once I understood the mechanics of the hovering flaw, ways to correct it became more apparent and more successful. Longitudinal flexing exercises, such as the series of transitions I practised on the second hovering horse, can work, if the rider can get the horse to work the joints of the hind leg and set the balance more toward the rear. However, if, as in the third hovering horse I tried to train, the movement has become habitual, and the inflexibility of the stifle is really confirmed, then transitions will not be very effective. It will be too easy for the horse to bounce the croup up in the downward transition rather than to flex in the hip, stifle and hock, and 'dampen' the step. The trainer will have a difficult time loading the haunches without great force, which is not the way for an *ecuyer*.

Much more effective is the use of proper lateral exercises, in particular the shoulder-in but also the renvers and half-pass. The shoulder-in has great value as a unilateral exercise. In the left shoulder-in, the rider/trainer can work specifically on the joints of the left hind and this specific loading can make a particularly stiff leg more flexible. Also by working one side at a time in a curve, the rider can arrest the attempt of the horse to stiffen the back, which is certainly what Seunig noticed. The half-pass becomes an enigmatic exercise because it has different effects depending on how shallow the rider traverses sideways. In a fairly straight, shallow half-pass in which the horse is properly bent around the rider's inside leg, the horse's inside leg will work up under the curved body and take up a good deal of loading. As the half-pass moves more radically to the side, and stays parallel to the wall, this demands more cross-over by the hind legs. There is going to be a reverse relationship to loading and the outside leg will have to become more and more prevalent to push the mass of the horse over to the side.

When one sees radical half-passes performed at the Spanish Riding School, one always sees considerable angle in the horses. The shoulders are quite a bit ahead of the hindquarters. The horses are not kept parallel to the wall as one sees in competition horses. The result of more angle is an insurance that the horse will stay classically bent and more loaded on the inside leg and not turn the movement into a flat-out traverse with much cross-over and more push from the outside leg.

By understanding these effects and then using combinations and repetitions of these exercises, I found I could interrupt the habitual pattern of the flawed gait. Secondly because of their ability to work specific sets of muscles unilaterally, I could build strength and flexibility more or less on one side or the other. Thirdly, by frequent changes from left rein to right rein, one has a barometer to compare the sides of the horse, thereby checking development. Finally, by curving the body of the horse, not the neck, repeatedly in rein changes from left to right exercises, the back becomes more flexible laterally and longitudinally along with the joints of the legs.

The hovering trot is a muscular problem. Like most ways of going, predisposition to it is probably genetic. However, the trainer can make headway if he realises the sites at which the work must take place: namely, the stifle, hip, hock and shoulder. Then he needs to apply creatively the traditional exercises to develop flexibility and strength in those areas.

In my impudent challenge of the great horsemaster, I learned something else: that almost all descriptions that become frozen by words are usually on their way toward becoming something else. This is what I alluded to in the introduction. During the Journey the horseman may arrive back at a city where he has already been and find that the city has changed. Beneath one civilisation lies another and another. The Buddhist master used to say that the student must stand on the shoulders of the teacher in order to see farther. Every learning person builds his case as solidly as possible, not to hold it in eternity by its great construction, but to serve as an honourable base well built for something to go on top of it.

In the development of the technical, there are two things going on. One is a pragmatic procedure, brought about by trying to do something quicker, smoother, more efficiently – the world of logical physical development.

Simultaneously, one's mind is in a floating mode. Even in, and perhaps especially in, ritualised practice, one is aware of another world – the world of the psyche, the creative world, the world of change. Only in this world can new development come out. Only by tapping into this world is any adaptation possible.

Seunig's words are not really wrong any more than mine are right. What they really become are sort of constructs like poems, which encourage by their existence the process of looking. Only by really looking can you really ride.

Chapter Three

Rockin' and Rollin' in the Passage

I ONCE HEARD a painter explain that after he had worked on one painting for a long time, he would find he got a little blind to his work. When this happened he would often look at his painting through a mirror. In this simple inversion the painting would be revitalised for him, and with this fresh vision he would see all kinds of things he wanted to work on. Very often I have learned my greatest lessons about certain movements by dealing with flaws that prevented me or a particular horse I was training from accomplishing them. In trying to correct some of the inversions, or faults, in the training of passage, I began to see more and more what the passage was not. The mysterious, beautiful passage defined itself as I cut through layer after layer of the disguises of evasion.

BALANCÉ

Whenever I go to horse shows I am always drawn to the warm-up areas – even more than to the actual finished performances or exhibitions. On one particular day I was at an international horse show watching several horses warm up. A young man and his horse began to practise passage. As they warmed up the horse was trying harder and harder. The young man was being coached and after a bit the coach kept saying, 'Balancé. It's balancé. You must ride the horse more forward. More forward!' He spoke louder. The more the young man tried, the worse the balancé got. I could not help but empathise with the young rider. I had been in his position, and when the passage gets into stronger and stronger balancé, it can feel like you are riding an octopus with legs reaching out in every direction. It had been at least ten years since I had first ridden the passage on the Lusitano horses of Portugal, who were masters of the air. I know that I did not realise at the time how sublime this experience was. Nor how long it would take to be able to train a horse myself to do a passage even near that expressive. Nor how many ways one could go wrong.

So what is this balancé (bal/un/say) and will riding more forward help? If so, why?

When the trainer at that show implored his student to move the horse more forward to correct the passage, his advice was hardly unique. Yet it was not working. Riding the passage more forward (i.e. getting more engagement behind) is the proposed cure for practically **all** problems of the passage. A review of much of the riding literature

[36]

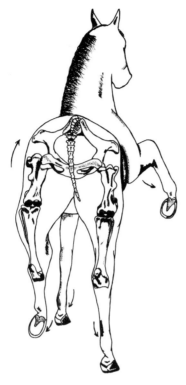

Fig. 3 The balancé in passage – the front leg action is exaggerated when compared to the hind leg action.

will also attest to this. I have found precious little advice on correcting the problems of balancé, or rolling in of the front legs, or swinging hind legs, etc. When I have asked many trainers to tell me why they think riding the horse forward works, it is usually a similar answer that the hind end is not carrying enough load, or it is being too inactive. Yet why do so many problems of passage manifest themselves in the odd action of the front limbs. To summarily dismiss the balancé as a problem of the hind legs was just too easy. So I went back to the scientists to study movement again and again, and little by little the motion revealed itself.

The balancé has been described as a circus passage. In general, when a horse passages in balancé, the front leg action is exaggerated as compared to the hind leg action. Furthermore the traditional description is also that as each front leg lifts into and through its exaggerated position it does not move straight but moves over to the side. The result is that the horse seems to sway from left to right and vice versa. For me the key descriptive identifier of balancé is that in the stance phase of each front leg, the hoof will be placed away from the horse's body (see Fig. 3), stretched out over its respective side. The left foot will reach out over to the left and the right over to the right. Whenever a horse starts to widen its stance, it usually is trying to widen its base of support. There is a physical rule which states that for an object to remain upright, a line drawn down from its centre of gravity must fall within its base of support. If the horse starts widening its stance on either front leg or hind, that can be the tip-off to where the horse is trying to carry the load.

The first matter to consider is how is this possible, since this kind of movement is unique to the front limbs. The front limbs have this greater facility for sideways motion because in the front legs there are no bony attachments to the trunk of the horse.[13] This allows for a lot of room for muscular adjustment, and therefore, muscular effect.

Even though the front limbs are primarily constructed for receiving force, as we have already noted, it is often forgotten that they can also generate considerable force. In the balancé the horse is deliberately using the forelimbs to help propel itself upward into a passage. In their effort to extend and propel forward they also generate sideways force. In a passage where the horizontal forward force is restrained and the upward vertical force is accented, the sideways force can be substantial. When the left front pushes off, extending through the second half of the stance phase, it forces the shoulder and trunk sideways, at which point the right front limb reaches out and plants itself to block sideways push, and returns it over to the left with its own extension. The front legs then are bouncing the horse's centre of gravity from side to side, as well as vertically up for passage. Forward riding at that point can eliminate the balancé because it re-establishes the horizontal forces of the trot and takes the emphasis off the vertical forces which define the passage. However, although forward riding may eliminate balancé, it might not necessarily help the horse's passage. He must learn to handle these vertical forces.

Although it is true that the hind end needs to carry more weight, that the centre of balance must be shifted more onto the hind legs with better engagement and better flexion, I think it is a real mistake to assume that the horse is not working in balancé and therefore needs to be pushed more. When the rider at the show in the beginning of this chapter tried to drive the passage more forward the horse only exaggerated the balancé. In my experience I have found that in balancé the horse may be working very hard, but he is working the wrong end, if you will. The horse can be confused and needs to be calmed down. The balancé showed me how a horse can try to balance its weight, to try to show a passage, but it is a passage that keeps the stifle and hock from doing the greater work. This does not mean that the horse is categorically lazy. It is my feeling now that, again, more forward riding can eliminate the balancé because it re-establishes the horizontal forces, but we need the vertical element in order to display real passage. In my opinion the cure lies in more fundamental collection. If the rear end and abdomen of the horse is systematically prepared and gets stronger and more flexible, it will be

[39]

able to carry more weight. The attempt can go too far, though, if the trainer crouches the horse too far down and forward with the hind legs. They can be cramped and will actually lose carrying power. Once the collection is cleaned, then and only then, will the horse be able to attempt passage without the over-zealous help from the front limbs.

There are, of course, many ways to develop and improve collection with more flexion and extension in the hock, stifle and hip. Some of these exercises are three hundred years old and still relevant. 'Trotting and stopping a horse is the foundation of all airs. They settle his head and croup and put him well up in his haunches and make him light before.' – Duke of Newcastle.[3] Progressive transitions develop flexibility and carrying power. Short-trot-to-walk transitions and vice versa, walk-to-soft-piaffe steps, longer-trot-to-collected-trot – all of these have a similar effect, of which Newcastle knew so much.

I think work in hand is also very useful in developing the action and strength of the stifle and hock. This is especially true in the early stages because, being an unmounted exercise, it is easier for the horse to find its own newer balance over the rear.

Perhaps the most important thing to remember in all these exercises, is that in order for them to have the desired gymnastic effect, the rider must use as little hand as possible. This not being the case, the horse will be blocked from using its neck properly, and also the horse may tip onto the forehand due to the hand's braking effect. The transition, especially downward, needs to be controlled by the rider's back, seat and leg. At the moment of the downward transition, the hands become passive but the rider almost holds the horse forward with his back and abdomen pressed toward the pommel. The upper body stretches tall so that the rider does not lean back. The thighs close to give strength to the back and to help absorb some of the roughness that is bound to occur when young horses are learning transitions. The experienced rider of young horses will dissipate some of the shock of the transition throughout the upper leg. This does not mean so much grip that it holds the rider up off the horse. No. It is a commonsense adjustment to keep the young horse from hollowing through the downward transitions, which would have an opposite effect of building a round horse. The rider keeps the driving aids on to teach the horse to go through the transitions, to carry itself behind and not throw itself on the forehand. This is done with constant repetitions. The joints of the rear will then develop more flexibility and strength until it is capable of sinking under and holding itself in balance in soft but powerfully flexible transitions. Finally, the horse develops such strength and flexibility that it will be able to propel the centre of gravity more upward as in the passage without needing the assistance of the front legs. Without the force of the front legs, the balancé will disappear. This I know from experience.

ROLLING IN AT THE PASSAGE

Another deviant relative of the passage is one that is again most noticeable in the action of the front legs. It can be seen in the passage when the front legs roll toward each other with the hooves being placed on the ground closer and closer to each other. In some of the worse cases the hooves will land during the stance phases under the chest in the same single track or even criss-cross to leave two tracks on the ground, but of the opposite legs! At first glance this seems to be the flip side of balancé. However, rolling in embodies the complexity of certain evasions and exposes the necessity of having to look at evasions holistically. The rider needs to keep an open mind lest he forces the horse into what he thinks is proper movement.

Between the shoulders and the hips of the horse, the individual vertebrae of the spinal column form a linked bridge. The bottom of those vertebrae make an upward curve, and in a very real way, the trunk hangs off this great arch. It is important to remember that it is the bottom of the vertebrae that form the upward curve because a look at the top-line of the horse can be deceiving. Since the vertebrae of the withers and then again at the hips are higher, it gives the appearance of the back sinking down when in fact it is actually curved upward, forming a strong arch. The muscles of the back can stiffen this arch so that propulsion generated by the rear legs will drive straight up through the shoulders and forward with the most efficient horizontal force. The opposite effect is like that found in the sophisticated bumpers of modern cars. Upon impact or force, the bumper is designed to continuously collapse, absorbing the impact force and dissipating it to deaden the rigid shock and absorb the energy. For the maximum horizontal movement the horse's back does not want to absorb and deaden the propulsion of the rear. It wants to relay it forward through its strength and firmness.

We know already from our look at the hover trot, that the passage will require some transfer of the efficient horizontal push into the more dramatic, albeit less efficient, vertical push. Imagine, then, as the left hind pushes off powerfully for passage, sending the horse less forward but more upward in great suspension, there will be a forward or horizontal force and an upward or vertical force. If the back of the horse is too weak and disconnected the upward force of the left hind pushing off the ground will throw the left hip upward and set off an axial twist* (see Fig. 4). Since its force is greater than its diagonal partner, the right front, the body of the horse will turn during suspension, forcing the right shoulder to dip down and the right legs to swing under the chest. In this kind of rolling there is good impulsion and engagement but the back of the horse needs strengthening so it will act more normally as in standard forward trotting. There the epaxial muscles etc. resist the torque and keep the horse level. Round transitions and shoulder-ins can help to stretch and strengthen such backs.

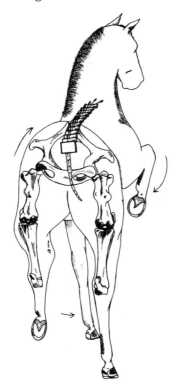

Fig. 4 The effect of a weak or disconnected back in passage (see text).

*For more information on axial rotation, see Leach paper, 'Kinematics of the equine thoracolumbar spine', Townsend, H.G.G., Leach, D.H., and Fretz, P.B., *Equine Veterinary Journal*, 1983, 15(2), 117-122.

Fig. 5 Front view of rolling in passage.

There can be another kind of rolling in: where there is little engagement from behind. The horse is not carrying the movement more on the hind legs and the centre of gravity is too far forward towards the shoulders. In an effort to help support the passage, the front limbs swing under the torso toward the centre of gravity in the middle of the body to support the overburdened forehand in their stance phase (see Fig. 5). This rolling in is a sort of flip side of balancé. Obviously exercises to correct this kind of defect will differ from the first rolling in. Here the horse needs more collecting and engagement to achieve more carrying power. More carrying power in the hind legs will free up the front limbs from their support work so they can travel out straight again.

Rolling in can be further complicated by actions of the head and neck of the horse, which can account for five per cent of the horse's bodyweight. Even slight deviations in the carrying or movement of the head and neck can have a drastic effect on the limb travel of the horse.

Stiff shoulders which restrict forward reach of the front limbs can encourage inward movement which will have the same stance and swing time as a full passage – except that now the front leg does not swing out and forward, but it swings stiffly in towards the body. Here the shoulder-in can be very useful in developing more flexibility in the shoulder, and freedom in the torso.

Obviously there are also deviations in travel and use of the hind legs. For example, if the horse is in balancé with the front legs generating more vertical force than the hind legs, and if the back is twisting, one sees a reverse of the rolling passage (see Fig. 6). Namely, the front legs are standing wide and the shoulders bind up and twist the

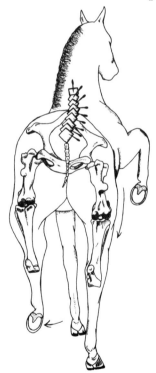

Fig. 6 Rear view of horse in balancé, but with an additional problem –
he is exhibiting an action that is the reverse of the rolling passage (see text).

opposite hip down causing that hind leg to roll under. The problem is dual: firstly, the centre of gravity is too far forward on the front legs; and secondly, the back is not solid and is lacking in resilient strength. When a passage has this much wrong with it, the horse needs fundamental work, and I think is categorically in over its head. The efforts to passage have to stop until better collection can be maintained together with flexibility. Flexibility in collection demands great strength from the horse and this kind of muscular development takes time. Fortunately there are many riding books, old and new, which carefully list and describe the whole transition of these traditional exercises and in the proper order of training.

In general, exercises which combine deep work and collection will develop strength and flexibility longitudinally. I think one always needs to keep in mind longitudinal exercises, be they collecting or stretching. These need to be done with the spine and top-line in extension. If the neck gets above the bit and shortens, or it gets below the bit and shortens, the effect can be the same: the back vertebrae fully flex or become hollow the moment this occurs. Roundness is lost. The hind legs get locked out behind because of the pressure on the top-line. Without good roundness and reach under by the hind legs, all transitions will fail. This is why one can see horses who passage hollowly, stop and make themselves round before they can go into piaffe. You might get away with a hollow passage and a hyperflexed back, and you might even get away with a hollow piaffe, but you will not get through the transitions of passage into piaffe. If the hind legs are camped out behind, they cannot come smoothly up a little more for the piaffe. If the horse is already round in the passage, then to become a little rounder for the piaffe is not deadly.

There are certainly many more deviations of the hind limbs but some of them I feel are better exposed in the piaffe. However, I think it is very important for the rider/trainer to have a system for investigating these deviations and then developing a knowledge of the traditional exercises which can be applied to specific weaknesses or flaws. As I have tried to show, blanket corrections such as riding forward can be too general to eradicate some of the idiosyncratic evasions that will develop if one trains more than one horse. As I alluded earlier it was in the struggle with these evasions, the feints of the false passages, that the real passage began to solidify before me.

MORE THOUGHTS ON PASSAGE

In the hover trot, the horse bounces its centre of gravity up and down. Its lazy forward motion is propelled seemingly only by tendo-ligamentous action. Muscle flexion and extensions of the stifle, hock and shoulder seem to be minimal.

In the balancé the horse is energised by the rider, but the centre of gravity is towards the shoulders and as the horse throws its weight vertically up with its front legs in an attempt to passage, it also pushes its torso to the side. The horse's centre of gravity is bouncing up and down, but it is also bouncing in the third dimension – sideways, left and right. The stifle and hock are carrying less weight than the shoulders.

In the rolling passage, the horse can be often well energised. The stifle and hock are extending and flexing exuberantly. There is good forward and vertical force, but the back and shoulders break apart. The horse begins to twist through the bridge of its back so that when the left hind pushes up, it forces its diagonal partner, the right front, down and under, and vice versa.

There is often much talk about propulsion in the passage – all this great thrust. My feeling is that this kind

[47]

of language is better suited to describe the extended trot. The passage reveals its trademark in its conscious adjustment of the muscles which flex the hips, stifle, hock and shoulder, and pull this trot up in the air with an equally great horizontal and vertical extension. It is not the stiff recoil off the pasterns like the tendo-ligamentous hover trot which is simply reflexive. No. It is a conscious interruption of the simple reflex, a controlled exhibition of the greatest and smoothest joint flexion and extension. It is a display of trained flexibility and strength. The spine of the horse is supported at two places: one, at the forelegs and shoulder; and the other at the sacroilliac joint in the hind legs. Any area in between these two connections can twist, especially when moving.[13] In the passage the back muscles do two things simultaneously: they must be strong enough to transmit the considerable forward force of the passage, and absorb the twisting effects due to the vertical forces generated by the hind legs. The back must be flexible enough to swing and even bend as in ultimate passage on two tracks. Since the passage is principally a two-time gait with the same stance and swing time, the shoulder then, although not necessarily matching in propulsion, must match the rear in flexibility.

What makes the passage so difficult is its requirement for great flexibility in the joint of the limbs, and great strength to deliberately interrupt the reflexive trotting stride, which has a more horizontal force, and consciously extend the stifle early so that it sends the horse more upward with less horizontal force and more vertical force. All this must occur without any major lateral deviation of the limbs' travel direction. Finally, it must be symmetrical and even, regardless of which diagonal pair is doing it. To accomplish this, the horse must be gymnastically prepared over a relatively long period of time, and tested slowly. The trainer has to be careful to avoid over-working the movement. As soon as the horse stops carrying the load behind, or loses its balance, evasions will appear. This is especially true in a game horse or an ambitious trainer. Even though a horse may be mentally ready, the work has to go slowly because it takes much longer for the musculature to develop over the comprehension. It is my feeling now that the great majority of evasions are the result of muscular inadequacies with the game horse. Unable to execute the strenuous passage, this horse tries to compensate and the dull trainer forgets to interrupt.

In general the passage is trained in one of two broad systems. The first and most traditional and popular is to train the passage out of the piaffe. In this system, the passage will be developed by lengthening the great collection of the piaffe. The centre of gravity is already well set back toward the rear. If the trainer advances this piaffe rhythm judiciously forward, he can keep the balance more toward the rear because careful acceleration will keep the weight back. This will avoid falling into many of the balancing problems that occur when the balance gets too far out over the front legs.

There is a funny thing about the piaffe-to-passage transition. If the trainer allows the horse to jump into the passage and change the shape of its back, i.e. become too flat, he may get away with it on the transition upward. But he will pay for it when he tries to make the transition from passage back to piaffe. The horse, as I have said, will not be able to round the back without first stopping the passage and then regenerating the piaffe which always seems faulty.

The second broad system is to train the passage by restraining the extension forces. By holding in a medium trot, compressing the horse at the urge to extend, when the horizontal forces are dammed up, the force gets

[49]

transferred up and vertically into the suspension of passage. This system, which works through restraining forces, has built into it a serious pitfall. Namely, the braking forces inherent in any restraint can tip the balance forward onto the shoulders and off the haunches. Knowing what we do about balancé it takes a little imagination to see that it is easy to develop front-end deviations if too much weight is being carried by the forehand. Furthermore if the horse gets used to the suspension of passage with its balance more in the middle, it can be very difficult to get the horse to settle back on its haunches in piaffe out of passage, and learn the passage-piaffe transitions.

If the horse is already in a proper passage, the balance will be on four legs, but a little more toward the rear. The transition from passage into piaffe will require the moving horse to shift the balance even farther toward the rear. This is especially difficult while moving forward with some horizontal force. It takes great strength and even more flexion and extension in the hock than that already being shown by the horse. There is also a risk when shortening the passage to use the reins and to stiffen the back, which, as we already have seen, can lead to rolling. It is a transition of great demands. This is the reason why, in general, trainers have preferred to train the passage out of the collection of the piaffe.

There are always exceptions with horses, and flexibility in training regimens is the hallmark of a good trainer/rider. In any case I think General Decarpentry's advice is worth nothing:

'In whichever order the passage and the piaffe are obtained, the trainer's big difficulty will always be the transition from one to the other, the perfect 'blending' of the two which is the major part of the artistic value of these movements as a whole . . .'[14]

He goes on to say that this is a good reason to start 'conventionalising' the trot at both ends simultaneously, i.e. start passage and piaffe at the same time. I think this is good advice.

Some years ago a controversial project to restore Michaelangelo's painting in the Sistine Chapel was undertaken. In great privacy, using space-age techniques, the most careful process of washing began. When it was finished, by all accounts there was a spectacular difference. Flesh tones that had faded to grey were now restored as if to life. The paintings' original colours were astonishing. Then the most amazing thing happened. Many great authorities of art hated it. There was a barrage of criticism – some of it highly intellectual, some instinctive. Obviously many 'experts' had come to like the artwork dirty and dull. Maybe in its darkened amorphous state they had more room for their own interpretations, more room to make it their own. Over a period of time, even the most sophisticated opinions had trouble holding their voices – because it was clear above everything else that Michaelangelo did not paint it overcast in grey and brown. In the end, every arguer, no matter how powerful, political, dogmatic, erudite or clever, had to stand in front of Michaelangelo himself and tell him why his own creation was somehow lacking in its original colours.

Every horse has a passage in its own original colour. The way I see it, the best trainers 'wash' the movements of the developing horse over and over to take off filtering affectations, to find the original, the natural, the real. But there has always been a class of trainers who set themselves apart because of their erudition, charm, sophistication or power. They are like the art critics. They need to make the horse's movements their own.

They seem always to want to do better than the natural and original. If you train a horse this way, always trying to add something, instead of washing something off, you can lose the dignity of the original horse, whichever one you are working with.

You have forgotten why you are riding, and someday when you are telling the horse how he must move, you will have to stand in front of him and convince him that Michaelangelo could not really paint either.

Chapter Four

The Piaffe

ONE SUMMER, through a twist of fate, the dressage rider and trainer John Winnett came to the area where I live. Eventually, and for a time toward that winter, he kept his horses at our stable. John was one of the most experienced international competitive dressage riders in the United States. At the time we each had a chestnut coloured Grand Prix horse and we were asked to try to prepare a Pas de Deux. John was always helpful to me and I enjoyed his company.

John was raised in France and by his own admission began riding in a Baucherist tradition. Later he knew and worked with many of the top German riders and trainers, having spent years living and competing in Germany. This fascinated me and I always wanted him to pursue these differences and similarities in his writings and conversations – especially from a historical sense. I thought his situation was unique and his perceptions valuable. I was curious as to his ideas and how he synthesised these apparently different approaches into his own dressage. Having sat through several meetings that concerned American dressage, engaged in lengthy discussions with him, I think John got bored with those endless historical arguments and I remember he almost chided me that we had come a long way from Baucher and Guérinière.

It was that statement that came to my mind when I was walking into the library at New Bolton Center, the famous large animal hospital and equine research facility of the University of Pennsylvania. New Bolton is only three miles from our farm. It is set right in the middle of some old horse country. This evening it was snowing as I drove by the post and railed pastures on either side of the road. There were no other cars as I passed the old brick and stone farmhouses and the horses. The Jean Austin Dupont Library is housed in a research unit at New Bolton. I walked into the warm building. It was quiet inside. During part of the winter when students come out from the city campus, the library is open at night. There are rarely more than a few people there and the research folk are usually gone.

As I walked down the hall it was shadowy, lacking the brightness of the daytime lighting. State-of-the-art machines hummed. I passed by rooms for 'Microbiology Research'; heavy doors warning: 'BIOHAZARD – Extremely Infectious Agents Inside'; locked doors with elaborate time-clocks; autoclaves; sterilising rooms; rooms for medical research. The office for 'Cytogenetics' had a board outside naming some of the breakthroughs in identifying chromosome abnormalities. I felt I was in some space-age cell which had entered a quieter pause for the evening. This is a place where searches take off into the unknown; where excitement emanates from even the most obscure discoveries – even the potential for discovery. Always there is the sound of beautifully wierd and specific machines of high science.

I had come to read from two old volumes of the Duke of Newcastle's (William Cavendish) *A General System of Horsemanship in all Its Branches*. It is over three hundred and fifty years old. At New Bolton, The Fairman Rogers Collection contains a magnificent assemblage of historical equestrian masterpieces. These are kept under lock and key and I have been given permission to study them in the library.

When I walked into the small modern library, the irony of this place and John's words came poignantly to life. On the left side of a small aisle are the wood and glass cases which house the works of Guérinière, the Duke of Newcastle, Pluvinel, Baucher, Seeger, and hundreds of leather-bound treatises. On the right are stacks of the most current research articles published in veterinary journals, and magazines, books and records of conferences. In some ways a step across that three-foot aisle could traverse hundreds of years of horsemanship.

At times it is difficult to place this distance in perspective. For many people that aisle of just three feet can represent an impassable chasm. To some modern horsemen the literature on the left is archaic, antique and useless. To some other old-fashioned horsemen, horsemanship has not advanced since these writings. For these horsemen the equitation of today is a pure regression from those earlier times.

Tonight the library is practically deserted, and there is

something in this chilly winter evening that plays on my mind in a melancholy way. As I stare at the physically small space of the aisle, I realise that all the writer-riders to the left are dead. Whereas, to the right most of the writers are alive. It isn't a morbid feeling that I have, just weighty, sombre. I am thinking about all the great thoughts there, the lessons, the calibre of these horsemen. I dwell on the idea of the words on the pages – as each one was written it became fixed in time and space; it has no chance to grow anymore. New explanations, even by the same writer, will need new words. So the written word cannot grow as can the man or woman who wrote it, but neither can it grow old, as can its author. It is a strange deal: the immortal but fixed word, and the mortal but moveable man. When I look at all the books and words of Guérinière, Pluvinel, Newcastle, Steinbrecht, Baucher, Grisone, all right there, it is like seeing a great equestrian graveyard. And yet, from any study of these words, one sees how one horseman picked up the dead words of another and moved them in some way. So the seemingly stiff and unchangeable words may become enhanced or they may be abused – but they are moved.

Ideas have moved on and fanned out like a river at a delta. Rivulets wind and dry up, or wind and rewind, or wind and rejoin. Wherever you stand in your time, if you turn around and look back at the delta, you know that back there through the thousands of twists and dead-ends is the same source. The journey back on this river of words sometimes dries up in the archaic – like an unadaptable species, it becomes extinct. But then in others the source is vibrant and pulsing. At these moments Guéninière can come alive for you. Pluvinel can point to something just for you. You feel the attitude of the Duke of Newcastle as if you, yourself, were being rebuked.

[56]

The Piaffe

No matter what some people would have you believe, that river of words has never stopped and it does not stop at that aisle in this library. It isn't easy to follow it sometimes. Like desert streams which can go underground to surface surprisingly in another part of the country, these rivers of words can go underground, disappearing seemingly without trace, only to surface again, sometimes in an archaic form and sometimes amazingly current. It is worth the trouble to try to follow these courses. It is in these always-moving rivers of information, these lineages of knowledge, that many of the answers to the problems of training horses lie. Great riders have told you something. They thought it was important.

Sometimes the movements that we train reflect the forces of vibrancy, and sometimes the forces of extinction. A movement like 'aubin'* is not seen any more. Even 'terre à terre'†, although it is still performed in France, is almost extinct. If the modern horseman were to read Pluvinel without help, he might not know what kinds of movements the master is talking about. But the piaffe! There is vibrancy. The piaffe travels right across that aisle easily. Everybody knows about the piaffe, don't they?

Before we look at the mechanics of this movement, there is an important introductory perspective that has to be mentioned. It later explained to me how it is possible for there to be so much confusion about what constitutes a good quality piaffe among some apparently knowledgeable modern horsemen.

It has to do with the use of the piaffe, if you will, because there is a considerable difference between its past use and its common use today. I call these differences

---

* *aubin* = canter in front, trot behind.
† *terre à terre* = a kind of rocking back and forth from both front legs to both hind legs.

Piaffe as Preparation, and *Piaffe as Culmination*. In the past, even though the piaffe was practised as an 'air' in itself, as was *terre à terre*, it was also the critical springboard for all the jumps or 'airs above the ground'. The piaffe, because of its collecting abilities, prepared the horse just before the moment of take-off, by getting the haunches to begin to pull the weight back and carry it on the hindquarters, thereby freeing the forelegs to come off the ground entirely. If you watch practice sessions at Saumur or the Spanish Riding School, you will see the exuberant horses often piaffing vigorously just before the set-up for a capriole or courbette. Sometimes *terre à terre* is also seen. In my opinion this is why one can still observe excellent piaffe at those places. It is not only because of the conformation and breeding of the horse, it is also because the jumps keep the piaffe honest. The forehand must be light and free because in a second it is going to come up entirely off the ground in a very specific and controlled jump executed entirely on the hind legs.

Today we mostly see *piaffe as culmination*. Very few people in the world still practise the airs above the ground. In competitions they are not allowed, and the piaffe is the summit of the FEI's requirements. The result is that today you can see complex evasions occuring in the piaffe, primarily because they are misbalanced in one way or another. Sometimes these piaffes are executed by clever horses, sometimes they are trained by clever riders. Nevertheless, they are the piaffes that score well in competitions and fulfil the requirements of the rules of competition. But they are piaffes that no horse could ever jump out of in a controlled way because they are not being carried by the hind legs and are balanced more towards the reins.

When you analyse the piaffe from its classical descriptions, you see a two-beat gait, a kind of trot in place or what has sometimes been called passage on the spot. Neither of these phrases is adequate. The harmony of the piaffe comes from the diagonal pairs of legs having approximately the same stance and swing time. The piaffe gets its rhythm from the left hind and right front staying on the ground for the same amount of time, then smoothly transferring to the other diagonal pair. What happens in the swing time is a very different story.

The traditional description, in general, is that piaffe allows for the hind foot of the horse to raise off the ground to the coronet band, or so. The exact place is not that important providing both hind feet raise to the same height along with the requirements of engagement. The front feet should raise up halfway up the cannon – sometimes more, sometimes less. What is important here is that the front feet have been traditionally asked to come off the ground approximately twice as high as the hinds. Now, if the stance time is the same for front and rear legs, it goes without saying that the swing time, the time in the air, must also be the same. Yet we have this requirement that during the same swing time, or same amount of time off ground, the front feet must travel twice as far (twice as high). It doesn't take a genius to realise that the front feet must therefore travel twice as fast as the hind ones. Then something important happens because one of the first requirements of the classic piaffe, contrary to a lot of opinion, is that it not be symmetrical front to back in spite of its sublime appearance. If you ask how this is possible, the first thing that comes up is that the haunches are carrying more load so the front legs will be more unencumbered. Relieving them of some of the weight-bearing duties, they will be able to travel faster. In this respect a classic piaffe should prove that the horse is carrying his weight with the hind legs and that the rider has mastered collection. It seems logical then to say that if a horse displays a piaffe with the front feet moving up to mid-cannon and the hind feet moving up to the coronet, and the diagonal pairs have the same stance and swing times, it must be a classical piaffe.

The answer is no. The reason is that some horses can stay in this rhythm, meeting these requirements, but they can hold the bulk of the balance on their front legs and even one front leg. Such a horse can show a deceptively low hind end and raise its front feet high, and yet hide from the first and most important requirement, namely that the piaffe show ultimate collection, i.e. that it is being balanced more on the rear legs. How can a horse or rider do this? One way is for the horse to 'triangulate'.

TRIANGULATION IN THE PIAFFE

One year I was given a gift of a clock for the stable, and on its face is a graphic silhouette of a horse in a piaffe. I have seen this particular shape of piaffe in countless advertisements and horse magazines. No doubt it seems like a great piaffe to the artist, to the many illustrators who draw it over and over again, and to many advertising people who use pictures of horses piaffing in this form. The hind legs are always well engaged under the horse. The croup seems deep set, with one hind foot in elevation, at least to the coronet band but usually higher. The front leg that is raised is high and proud. But the stance-phase leg is always pointed or slanted back toward the hind feet. In all its different versions the common denominator is that the front feet creep back toward the centre of gravity, and the hind feet creep forward, moving towards one another and forming the point of a triangle. The front legs form one side of the triangle, the hind legs form another, while the body of the horse forms the third

Fig. 7 Triangulation in the piaffe.

(see Fig. 7). When the horse begins to bring its front legs back from the vertical, it ceases to matter what is happening behind because even if it looks deeply engaged, it is false. The front legs are shifting back to get under the centre of gravity and to relieve the hind legs. This is the opposite of the classical piaffe, which demands that the hind legs carry the load.

The curious thing I have learned about this triangulation is that it is often caused by the over-zealous trainer, who in an effort to really load the haunches, pushes them *too* far under the horse so they become very cramped. When they become this stretched they have no room to flex, and, more importantly, the stance leg cannot extend properly because the centre of gravity always seems behind the hind legs. Remember that in the trotting stride there are two phases: the braking phase, where the hips flex upon the foot hitting the ground; then as the hips move over the foot, the propulsion phase takes over and

[61]

propels the centre of gravity which is falling downward, forward. If the hind legs are always too far forward of the hips, and the horse is held on the spot, the propulsion phase can't happen. The centre of gravity of the hind end must move forward over the leg, where extension can propel the weight vertically and horizontally. The horse, realising that it can't propel, shifts its front legs back to relieve the cramped hindquarters and, as in the balancé at passage, it uses its shoulders to help carry more weight. This is why the best riding masters always insist in training that the piaffe move forward a little. In triangulated piaffes, the haunches can be very deep set and the hocks very well flexed and yet be carrying almost no weight. Lowering the haunches does not necessarily mean that one has loaded them. This apparently deep-set piaffe is exactly the opposite of the classical piaffe in that it is actually carrying more weight on the shoulders and on the front legs. This is a classic example of *piaffe as culmination* – the piaffe looks all right, but a horse could never jump out of it without changing the balance.

Although clarification of this mechanism has come about through analysis of some very high-speed films and in through reviewing some current research in biomechanics, it is very clear that among knowledgeable trainers of *haute école* this problem of falsely deep-set haunches was known. The Duke of Newcastle[3] says that the whole study is to put the manège horse on the haunches, but that it is important to understand when the horse is really on his haunches and when not. He clearly explains that a horse can be almost sitting on his croup but will not be on his haunches if his hind legs are too distant from their normal and natural lines 'which is to have them (too) much asunder'. He then describes how the horse should have as much flexion, bending in the hock, as possible but the legs should not deviate from their normal position.

(Sometimes a horse that does a piaffe which, as French writers often say, resembles a passage on the spot – meaning the front and hind legs move closer in symmetry and the haunches don't sink excessively – can actually be more classical. This shows better collection even if the croup is a little higher than in a horse which shows a piaffe with a deeply set hind end but is holding it up with the front legs.)

There is a very good analogy for triangulation in human locomotion: when a person who has an injured hip walks and leans the upper body over the injured hip when that leg is in its stance phase – on the ground. By moving the centre of gravity toward the injured hip, the person reduces the moment (a product of quantity [as force] and the distance to axis) in the stance phase. Perhaps more simple put, he reduces the force on that hip in the stance phase. The triangulating horse moves the front leg back. Thus both human and horses are leaning or balancing toward their respective centre of gravity in order to reduce the stress or work of moving correctly in balance over all limbs. The curious thing is that in correcting the human's way of going, the physiotherapist will give the patient a cane for support – but in the oppsite hand! The therapist wants to establish the correct balance over two limbs. If one uses the cane on the same side as the injured hip it will allow the patient to put even more unbalanced weight over that side.

In this therapy lies the clue for correcting triangulation in the horse as well. Namely the trainer must allow and encourage the hind legs to back away from the front feet. Then, uncramped, they will be able to carry their share of the weight and relieve the front legs, which will also return more towards the perpendicular.

PIAFFE WITH HIND FEET TOO HIGH

When a horse piaffes with the hind feet high and loose, sometimes even raising them up higher than the front feet, we have a kind of mirror problem of cramped hindquarters which are 'too much asunder'. Here the hindquarters are not loaded either, but in a very different manner; and the front legs are still carrying the bulk of the piaffe. This flaw is easier to see because the hip of the horse bounces freely and stiffly up and down. There is an anecdote that when one of the riders at the Spanish Riding School wanted to demonstrate what real flexibility and elasticity in the piaffe meant, he had a glass of water placed on his horse's croup in the piaffe. The elasticity and flexion was so clean and smooth that there was not enough shock to spill the water. In the horse who piaffes with his hind feet too high the glass would be sent flying. This kind of action in the piaffe can be caused by inflexible joints in the hind legs. Sometimes it is conformational, as in horses who have a high croup and find it difficult to sink behind or to come under with their legs. This conformation is not necessarily the kiss of death. Even though these horses may be limited as to how much they can come under, if they are developed muscularly, the muscles of the abdomen, neck and back can compensate and still produce loading behind, even if the sinking is less noticeable. As I have said, these piaffes will look more like a passage on the spot, but they cannot be considered bad piaffes as long as they show real collection and good rhythm, especially in and out of piaffe-passage transitions.

If the horse that piaffes too high behind can be brought to do better piaffe, it will be done by increasing overall strength in the abdomen, neck and rump, but particularly the strength and flexibility in the hind legs. I think work in hand is excellent to show these horses how to engage more, initially without the weight of the rider. Once the behaviour, in a sense, is trained into the horse, and the horse understands, the new neuro-muscular pattern of loading the haunches then becomes a matter of repetition and progressive training exercises by the rider.

PIAFFE WITH THE HIND LEGS TOO CLOSE TOGETHER AND THE HIND LEGS TO FAR APART (THE LESSON OF LEVADE)

In order for an object to remain upright a vertical line projected downward from its centre of gravity must fall within the area of support. If the line falls outside this area, the object will topple over.

If you look at any picture of a horse in levade, its hind feet will be well placed under its body and they will be placed well apart from each other. The great muscle and ligament systems of the rump, abdomen and neck will be bristling as they pull the horse back and up over the legs. In the levade all weight is carried on the two legs of the hindquarters. The front end is suspended off the ground and held in balance. So if you reverse the above physical rule, and draw a line on the ground from hind foot to hind foot, and then draw another imaginary line up into the horse from the groundline between the horse's hind feet, it will go up through the horse's centre of gravity. The wider the feet, and thus the wider base of support, the more room for the centre of gravity to balance inside this area of support. The closer the horse's hind feet are together in the levade, the less the area or base of support and the more difficult it is to balance or stay upright. For the sake of argument if the hind feet were to move practically right on top of one another, it would be like trying to do a levade on a fence post; the base of support has dwindled down almost to a point. So when the line from the horse's centre of gravity moves even a little outside this point of support, the horse topples over or back down.

When the hind legs of the horse start coming very close together in the piaffe, you can assume that they are carrying less and less weight. Their area of support is very narrow and small because it is unnecessary. Most likely, this piaffe is balanced too far out on the forehand and needs more collection. Traditional collecting exercises are needed. Also in-hand work with a stiff, long whip, which can point to the legs and push them to indicate more engagement, is excellent to show the horse what we want.

When the hind legs of the horse are widening like in a levade stance it can signal that they are beginning to carry too much weight. I know some trainers who would say it is impossible to carry too much weight behind. These trainers love to see a piaffe that lives in the moment before levade. To me, this kind of piaffe is overdone and ostentatious. It is not a traditional or natural piaffe, because when the forehand is carrying almost no weight the piaffe can disassociate too much.

The difference in the speed that the front foot is travelling while in the swing phase and the speed that the rear diagonal partner is travelling can be so disparate that the piaffe moves farther and farther from the trot-like gait. So instead of the piaffe representing the ultimate culmination of collecting a trot, it becomes a gait of its own with the front feet travelling two or three times faster than the hind ones. To me, the piaffe has a certain responsibility to remain a trot-like gait. Furthermore, if the piaffe is set too deeply, teetering on the point of levade, it becomes difficult to make transitions from piaffe to passage and vice versa.

When the rider/trainer notices in training that the horse is getting too wide behind in the piaffe, he should encourage or allow the piaffe to go more forward. Then the hind legs will exhibit more extension and the front legs will resume a proper supporting role, but **only** the supporting role of purifying the diagonals – not of holding the horse up.

LATERAL DEVIATIONS IN THE PIAFFE

I am convinced from my experience that balancé in the piaffe is similar to balancé in the passage. It is a result of inferior collection and engagement behind. Nevertheless the spirited horse tries for the movement, helping with the front legs. Thrust from either front leg can have considerable sideways force, especially in the piaffe where almost all the energy is being sent vertically instead of forward (horizontally). The front end gets pushed from side to side as each front leg reaches out to block the lateral forces and sends the torso back up and over in a vicious cycle. I think the horse has to relax a little and go back to a highly collected trot or some less-pressured half-steps. When collection over the rear legs is perfected one can try for a more accented piaffe. Once the balance is back in order and the horse accepts the rein going through the body, the forehand will be lighter. Now, without the need to be doing what the hind legs were supposed to be doing, the front limbs stop driving so hard and raise up and down like yo-yo's, falling and rising straight from the trunk of the horse.

I believe that the flaw of rolling the front legs in towards a centre line, and even criss-crossing, in the piaffe is again similar to the same flaw in the passage – with the exception, as Podhajsky[15] has noted, that it can be even worse. As in the passage, if a very stiff back is not

absorbing the axial roll and a stiff shoulder is not allowing the front leg to flex and extend properly, the horse has
to move the front limbs when they are in the swing phase
(when they are airborne). If the shoulder is exceedingly
stiff it will not allow the leg to flex and extend nor the
foot to raise up and come back down in as straight a vertical path as conformation will allow. Instead it will swing
the whole stiff limb sideways – similar to a person with a
stiff knee who swings the leg in or out to move the leg
forward because the knee won't flex.

In the two worst cases of crossing over in front that I
have seen, both horses were standing wide behind. This
was perplexing to me at first but the more I understood
this flaw, the more logical this stance became.

We have already mentioned that a widened stance is a
tip-off in general that the horse is trying to carry more
load over those legs. Why are those horses that cross over
in front standing wide behind? Because unlike the balancé
where the front legs are doing too much to help balance
the piaffe, the stiff front legs are just swinging from side to
side – almost painfully avoiding flexion. If they are not
flexing up, they cannot possibly extend with any force
either. Therefore the hind legs are carrying the greater
proportion of the load. In rolling under, the front legs are
doing nothing to help balance and maintain the diagonals.
In balancé they are doing too much.

FEATURES OF THE TRADITIONAL PIAFFE

The piaffe is a movement in which the horse is moving its
diagonal limb pairs in the same stance and swing time
with very little forward advancement. In this trot-on-
the-spot of sorts, the front feet are required to travel
higher than the hind feet in the swing phase and therefore
must travel faster, which is what makes it different from

the trot. This is biomechanically possible because in the piaffe the horse has always been asked to move its centre of balance more toward the rear, deliberately disproportionately loading the hind legs and lightening the front. As well as a development exercise in itself, traditionally the piaffe was often used to coil the horse over its hind legs to prepare it to jump off the hind legs in one of the airs above the ground, as already described.

While the horse is in the piaffe it should exhibit little or no lateral deviation. We now know that many of these lateral deviations in limb travel expose weaknesses in the horse's ability to collect itself and to hold itself in balance. These weaknesses, when they can be fixed, need to be corrected at the most fundamental levels. Odd placements of legs need to be analysed to determine if more collection is needed, or more flexibility in the back, etc. Of course, it is always easier if these faults are noticed early and are not allowed to become engrained. Many good trainers have often suggested it is all right to let the horse carry its head a little lower in the beginning of piaffe training to allow the horse to use its neck in the initial difficult attempts to move into piaffe, and to ensure that the horse stays round and does not lock up in the back. I think this is also good advice.

Although the horse in piaffe should be fairly static laterally, that is, not swaying, the most experienced trainers have always suggested and insisted that it not be static longitudinally: that the horse be allowed to move forward. Again, from the mechanical point of view this makes absolute sense. Allowing the horse to move will ensure that there is flexion and extension of the hind limbs. It is this extension that moves the horse forward. It is also this extension which insures the complementary flexion thereby gymnasticising the hind legs. Only in a circuit of flexion and extension of the hind limbs will the trainer avoid cramping the hind limbs – as Newcastle would say, 'too much asunder' – with a falsely lowered croup and a horse falsely on its haunches.

It should be remembered that when the piaffe is held on the spot, in order to polish it, this is done as a finishing touch at the end of piaffe training. Very often this polishing has been done in hand or between the pillars. In the latter case it is almost always done unmounted. The inference seems clear. A piaffe performed without any forward movement is the most vulnerable to evasions, chiefly because it lacks the purifying factor of a complete cycle of flexion and extension, and is the most difficult to keep in balance. It can be polished and it can be destroyed when worked on the spot. In the end, the piaffe is an exercise. As a particular exercise it has the great abilities to strengthen the hind legs' carrying power as it calls into play the complete 'ring of muscle' – abdomen, neck, back and rump – and systematically develops them.

In the beginning of this chapter I was talking about fixations in time and space and about the progression of techniques and the sources of such progressions. If you read Guérinière you can see he credits La Broue and Newcastle as great influences. If you read Newcastle you can see the progression in technique in a movement like a shoulder-in, which is generally credited entirely to Guérinière. This goes on and on. One sees technique as a state of time, yet it does not describe the whole state of horsemanship. It can be argued, for example, that Leonardo Da Vinci's technology is inferior to that of today's average television repair man. Yet Da Vinci's artistry is timeless. It is so timeless, unfixed in space, that people still swear his paintings move. Newcastle's technology in his veterinary work, Volume 2, is inferior to the technology of today. His horsemanship is timeless. Inside a place in space and time one develops a quality unaffected by space-time. There are many serious scientists, and serious spiritual people, who say things like 'many realities lie side by side'.[5] If you can think only linearly, as in following the progression of technique, this concept is impossible to consider. Guérinière is dead and cannot speak to me now. However, if instead of thinking of the separate techniques of Xenophon, Newcastle, Pluvinel, Guérinière, you think of the artistry of each, a funny thing happens. You cannot place them in a neat and tidy progression. Instead, they stand side by side with their work, their art, in the same time – art time. In a very real sense, each one of us has to re-invent the wheel in our own time. What we must try to do is not necessarily re-invent the technological wheel with every generation, but we must re-invent the pyschological wheel, the artistic wheel, the psychic wheel. When one can find the wheel of the unconscious, Pluvinel comes back alive, and Guérinière has never died. You yourself come alive. By using the technological wheel correctly, you can move beyond it. You can see the source. You see your part as part of the source. You can see past the field of inferiority and superiority. You can be right there with Pluvinel now. The restraints of space and time are in your mind.

In the library, among the ghosts and words of all these great *ecuyers*, I see that this is no ordinary graveyard. Two things emanate from these ancient texts. One is technological and one is spiritual. They are equally real. One is sentence and structure requirements, description – the bone you might find in a grave. The other is the energy or spirit of a man. It hovers around the place where a person was, or the things a person made. Even when unrecorded consciously, it etches into and through the collective unconscious and it is very much present, real and available. The restraints are in one's own psyche.

[71]

I was beginning to see some of the limits of technological bravura, some of the traps on its measurements. In that same view I was beginning to get the signals of a way out.

Chapter Five

Deep Work

'. . . The first part [of practice] is loosening up and suppling the horse; second is work; third is riding dry. In the loosening-up phase, I try to set my horse long and low, meaning that the neck shall stretch forward and downward, so the horse loosens his back. During this phase, I don't watch so much the expression of the movements, but I do try to get rid of the stable exuberance and the superfluous drive to move, and to loosen up stiffness caused by standing in the stable, For me that is the loosening work – to ride my horse long and low during this phase.'[16]

Reiner Klimke
From an interview with Christian Thiess, *Dressage & CT Magazine*
Feburary, 1994

There are many trainers who do not use or believe in long and low or deep work. This seems more than anything to reflect a general past bias in the west towards muscular developments over tendo-ligamentus exercises. In many sports and some arts we have sought to develop more powerful and acrobatic athletes and the gains in muscle mass and strength have often been at the expense of flexibility. I say 'past bias' because I think most open-minded trainers have realised that a lot of current injuries are attributable to this system of training. Most athletes today are well aware of the importance of stretching in general and put important emphasis on it in training routines, especially in warm-ups. This is no different for the equine performer.

I have personally heard the rationale from dressage trainers that they can better raise the back of the horse through collection. Of course, one of the most basic requirements of collection is that the horse be round. The horse's head and neck must not be forcefully elevated so that the raised neck flattens the back down and forces the horse to go hollow. Instead, the horse is systematically prepared to engage behind and develop more carrying power on the hind legs through deeper flexion and extension. The abdominal muscles will gain strength and will add upward support for the back; as the belly contracts, the top-line extends. The neck will extend and raise, adding a kind of fulcrum torque over the withers, enhancing the back's lifting. Through a complex coordination the horse will become round, using his 'ring of muscle'. I would like to say one thing about the ring theory. As a pedagogical tool the 'ring' may have merit. However, in reality it is describing nothing less than how the whole body moves the horse. The complexity of this muscular activity cannot be underestimated. In 1978, Wentick, in looking just at the flexion and extension of the hind leg, analysed some thirteen active muscles, which clearly showed how complicated the muscle physiology can be.

Think for a second about opening and closing your hand. It is one thing to identify the components of the process, but then you have to apply them to actual situations of motion. For example, you can open your hand quickly and close it slowly, or open it slowly and close it quickly. The variations are infinite. All one has to do is look at the current technology involved in the design of human prostheses to get an idea of the mind-numbing complexities involved in the practical applications of the nuances of motion. It is my feeling that because of this complexity of muscle physiology one can sometimes get a better description of equine locomotion from a mechanical physicist's approach than from a biologically mechanical one. I think this is why you see such varying opinions when you talk to different biomechanical people. To this end I know there are some fascinating force-field instruments being built which are able to measure precisely the force exerted by certain limbs of the horse. It doesn't take much imagination to realise that this kind of work can actually prove or disprove some of the ideologies of dressage. At the least it will be able to show subtle differences in certain movements, i.e. whether a piaffe is on the forehand or not.

In general, the back of the horse is lifted, rounded, basculed in collection by complementary abdominal support, and by stretching over two fulcrums – one being the withers and the other being the lumbo-sacral joint. When the hind legs reach under, the great muscle-tendon ligament systems pull around the lumbo-sacral joint and lift the back like a see-saw. When the neck is stretched the dorsal and nuchal ligament system pulls on the spinal processes of the withers and the scaleni muscles at the base of the neck stabilise and push the lower neck up, the withers become another fulcrum so that the back lifts from the front also as the neck is stretched.[17]

Collection and deep work require vigorous activity behind. In collection, the abdominal muscles are used more and weight is being pulled onto the hind legs, so the forward motion or energy gets transported more vertically and less horizontally. The forehand is less encumbered because it carries less weight. Simultaneously the neck is carried higher but is still stretched forward in an uncramped arch. This retains an effective pull on the withers fulcrum, enhancing the round shape of the back even more. If the neck is cramped in an artificial arch or an arch that is too high and tight, the top-side of the neck will actually shorten, nullifying the fulcrum effect. Furthermore the underside of the neck will develop great muscles like goitres. Then the two ends of the horse begin working at cross-purposes. The first thing that suffers is the horse's back, which gets hyperflexed in its hollow form. There is then great stress on the stifle and hocks which are cramped out behind. This is what happens when you try to collect your horse with your hands. The horse becomes stiff with its back hollowed from restraining the neck.

So, in this complicated regard the back is of course lifted in collection. However, this requires a horse that is capable of collection. Therefore, the young horse is left out. Furthermore the warm-up becomes problematic because in order to have the back up you must start right away with collection. If not, your warm-up is hollow, and can be counter-productive.

The beauty of deep work is that it can be started with the horse whose back needs it the most, the young horse. Secondly, it serves as the ideal warm-up for the trained horse, because it is primarily a stretching exercise and helps keep the older horse flexible and free in its big gaits.

In deep work there are two principal schools of thought. Both require active forward movement behind, thereby fulfilling the fulcrum requirement over the lumbo-sacral joint and getting lift in the back in front of that joint. Differences lie in the position of the head and neck. In one school it is sufficient to have the horse's head low with the neck stretched. The nose of the horse may be pointing out. The fundamental requirement is that the neck be lower than the withers so that it satisfies the see-saw effect – when the neck goes down, the back behind the fulcrum of the withers goes up. The problem with deep work in this system is that it is possible for the horse to stretch but not along the crest; the nuchal system can be slack and the horse may be ewe-necked in spite of being low.

In the second school the horse needn't be as low in the neck but it can be. However, the horse should have more flexion – the nose must be in and the horse's head can even be slightly behind the vertical (see Fig. 8). If you

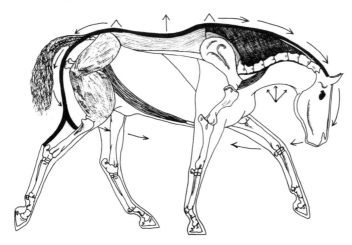

Fig. 8 Deep work. When correctly performed,
the back of the horse is lifted, rounded and stretched.

[77]

want to get a little feel for the difference, sit in a chair at your desk or table and lean forward slowly. Touch the flat surface in front of you with your chin. Next lean forward slowly again, and touch the table with your forehead. In touching with your chin, you can feel how straight your neck can be, even hollow, down to your own back. When you touch with your forehead, you can feel the stretch, the pull or curl all through the neck into the back.

When we work the horse in this second deep-work system, the crested neck ensures the stretching of the great nuchal ligament system along the top-line. When the horse is flexed slightly at the poll, this lever action adds a little more pull to this ligament system. It also helps to ensure that the horse, even when in a low-neck position, starts the cresting, or as Deb Bennett has said, the 'telescoping neck gesture' at the base of the neck where the scaleni muscles stabilise the underside of the neck and push up on the spine just above the chest. The lower neck, then, comes back and up and the crest seems to grow forward out of this base, and the spine extends.

This is fundamentally the same position the neck has in proper collection, as I have said, not elevated too high and tight, but reaching from the withers on top and from the base of the neck underneath toward the poll, which is at the highest point. Thus deep work in this shape has a very smooth and logical progression into the shapes of collection. What, in effect, changes between deep work and collection is not really the shape of the neck but the lowering or engaging of the hindquarters. In a real sense, the forehand does not levitate higher in collection; it is the hind end that sinks down. Of course, in collection the poll is up higher, but both exercises require an expansive extending spine and top-line. Only in that shape will the horse stay round in the back. Whereas when a horse is in flat, long and low, it will need to be 'put on the bit' and made round before it can move into collection. Dorso-ventral flexion must change into dorso-ventral extension.

The important thing is that the horse stretches out into an arch. Then even when the neck is low, it still maintains an arch. It is this arch which stretches the top-line of the neck into the withers and pulls the back up behind them. When this nuchal system is stretched, it acts like a spring[18] and with each step an elastic ripple can be felt. It is my opinion that the horse needs to be only slightly curved in order to be flexed at the poll to effect the elastic stretching. But it does need to be flexed. Sometimes the horse may be behind the vertical in the deep work. Yet when the haunches engage for collection, the forehand raises the same arched neck which will now assume the correct position of poll high and nose not behind the vertical. When correctly done, arched deep work can enhance the horse's natural movement and keep the horse flexible in the back and body so its stretching complements the later flexions of collection.

I also think it is very important that the deep work be done on as light a rein as possible for two reasons. One is that with the lightest of reins, the horse cannot seek support from the rider's hands. This will build big elastic gaits into the horse while emphasising self-carriage, even in a long and low position. This is very possible and in fact is easy to do. After a while the horse also develops psychologically and will stay responsible with complete freedom of the reins. The self-carriage and balance improves as well as the self-confidence.

The second and perhaps most important reason for riding this exercise with the lightest of reins is that the rider **will not force the horse into overbending or overflexing**, which can tear physical tissue and eventually have the exact opposite effect of stiffening a horse instead of freeing it. With light reins the rider can only suggest stretching and arching. The horse will seek a level of stretching it is capable of, which, over time, of course, should improve. The depth of the deep work should be determined by the horse and not the rider/trainer.

The deep work then is primarily a careful stretching regimen which stresses the long movement. It can develop self-confidence and self-carriage because it should be done with vigorous movement behind but with a very free rein. It is the antidote to bunchy or shortened gaits which can occur if the horse stays in collection all the time. It offers healthy counter-play to the physical demands of collection and makes sure that the rider keeps his horse elastic. When correctly used, the dorso-ventral extension of the spine in the deep work will be similar to the dorso-ventrally extended spine in collection. In the end, all this dorso-ventral extension or roundness is the only way to help the horse carry weight in the middle of its back, which is not something it comes by naturally. The millions of years of genetics in the horse's body type have not yet adjusted to being ridden. When weight is dropped on the horse's back without preparation, the horse's back will certainly flex and even hyper-flex to become hollow. To wander around without making an effort to round the horse's back is not kind. It borders on a kind of presumption that the animal will somehow adjust. The trouble is, of course, that most of the adjustments – high head, hind end out behind, short steps – are all detrimental to the horse's well-being. Deep work can help a horse not only to accommodate the rider but also actually enhance the natural movement of any riding horse.

Chapter Six

Lateral Work – In Search of the

Mother Load

MUCH OF RIDING knowledge is passed from teacher to pupil orally. Alois Podhajsky states in his book *The Riding Teacher* that 'the riding teacher should expect his pupil to follow his orders without qualification and to be willing to work hard in order to reach the goal set.'[19]

This statement goes beyond the obvious requirement of plain discipline needed in any learning situation. Since so much of teaching riding is the passing along of feelings and not just intellectual formulas, and since the novice rider has to learn to recognise the feelings with and without intellectual understanding, there is often a great deal of blind faith on the part of the student.

On the part of the instructor, it requires the carrying of a heavy ethical load. He/she must be responsible and thoroughly prepared in the lessons on any given day. He/she must continually upgrade his/her own knowledge with studently pursuit and an open mind. Where the student stops and the teacher begins is difficult to answer. Where faith must yield to the open mind and vice versa is impossible to answer.

When this process is at its best it can maintain its balance. However, because of strong loyalties and the transmission of feelings over facts, an unfortunate repercussion of this faith and trust can be a continued passing of incorrect information from generation to generation. Science can have a difficult road when trying to break into the tight traditions of horsemen. I think this explains why, in spite of conventional wisdom in the hundreds of systems for training the four classical lateral exercises – shoulder-in, travers, renvers, half-pass – the explanations, even from some outstanding expert sources, are contradictory and inaccurate. In some cases their use can produce the opposite effect of the one intended. However, there are some fairly simple biomechanical rules which I believe can clarify the forces involved in these exercises and thus advise the rider/trainer in their proper use.

Since the primary use of the bending exercises has to do with the asymmetrical loading of the hind legs for the purpose of conquering the natural asymmetry in all horses, it is imperative that the rider/trainer knows which hind leg exerts more force and is therefore doing more work or carrying more load, in which exercise. He/she can then try to develop more engagement of a deficient hind leg. When the hind legs have more equal engagement this will enhance collection and straightness.

In order to understand the mechanics of the lateral exercises, the first thing to realise is that if both hind legs propel the horse equally, the horse will move straight. In order for the horse to move off a straight line, one leg will have to exert more force than the other to lift the horse's mass and project it sideways, obliquely forward or on a bias, over the less loaded leg.

We have developed a simple rule-of-thumb to determine which leg is dominant. Whichever hind leg is crossing over, or in front of, the other, will be the limb that is exerting more force, doing more work, and carrying a greater load. The reasons for this is that it will always be that limb which will be directing the horse's line of travel. That limb will be the primary source of propulsion for the horse's mass in the line of travel. In spite of many assumptive explanations and theories, this rule holds true, regardless of the bend in any of these exercises.

For the sake of simplification, I will use the left bend in describing all these exercises and will consider all movement to be on three tracks. Riders and trainers can extrapolate from there.

In the **shoulder-in**, bent to the left, the horse is curved around the rider's left leg. The horse's line of travel, although relatively straight, will be on a bias left to right. The horse will leave three imaginary lines of tracks on the ground. (See Fig. 9.) The right hind travels forward by itself. The left hind travels forward on the same line as the right fore. The left fore travels forward on its own line. In the shoulder-in, bent left, the left hind steps over in front of the right hind. Its line of flight travels up under the belly of the horse. Of the two hind legs, it is the left which moves closer to the centre of mass and centre of gravity. Of the two hind legs it is the left hind which will

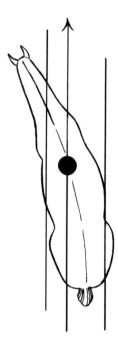

Fig. 9 Left shoulder-in. The left hind crosses in front of the right hind, closer to the centre of gravity. It is therefore the load leg.

exert more force, do more work and therefore harness more forces of load. The key to understanding the effect of these exercises is the line of travel. If the line of travel is left to right, obliquely left to right or even on a bias left to right, the left hind crosses in front of the right hind to step under the centre of gravity. This leg will be dominant in lifting the horse's mass and propelling it in the line of travel sideways. Remember, if both hind legs propel equally, the horse cannot move sideways.

In **travers**, bent to the left, the mechanics are identical to renvers. The difference between the two is only one of references to the wall and not in biomechanics.

In **renvers**, bent to the left, the horse will be bent around the rider's left leg. The horse will be travelling on a bias this time from right to left. The rider's outside leg will be slightly behind the girth encouraging the horse to move forward and towards the left. (See Fig. 10.) If we use the three imaginary tracks again, the left hind travels forward in the same line; the right hind travels forward in the same line as the left fore for the second line; and the right fore travels forward alone for the third track. In the renvers, bent to the left, the right hind steps up in front of the left hind. The right hind moves closer to the centre of mass and centre of gravity than the left hind which moves more off into space. The right hind lifts and propels the horse's mass from right to left. The right hind exerts more force, does more work and is the primary (i.e. load bearing) limb as it directs the line of travel off straightness and over to the left.

Fig. 10 In renvers bent to the left, the right hind steps over in front of the left hind, closer to the centre of gravity. It lifts and propels the horse's mass. It is therefore the load leg.

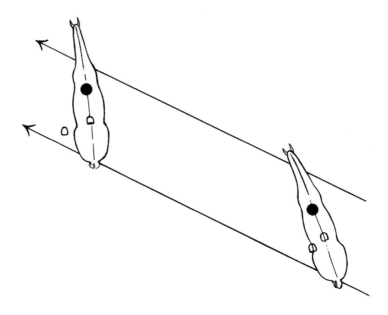

Fig. 11 Half-pass bent to the left. Depending on the angle the horse's body the exercise can be made more gymnastic (see text).

In Podhajsky's book, *The Complete Training of the Horse and Rider*,[15] he mentions that a popular gymnastic exercise at the Spanish Riding School is to move from the shoulder-in into renvers. Going from right shoulder-in, where the right hind is the inside leg but is the leg crossing up in front of the left, the rider changes the bend of the horse's body, but in fact the right hind still remains the leg that crosses over in front of the left hind. That this exercise is possible is due to that fact that, irrespective of bend, the right hind in this case continues from shoulder-in into renvers to remain directing the line of travel from right to left. It remains the leg that continues to exert more force and does more work.

The last of the four lateral exercises is the **half-pass**. It is one of the most interesting and points out the genius of some of the classical masters. In the half-pass, bent to the left, the horse will be bent around the rider's left leg and the rider's right leg will coax the horse forward and over to the left. The horse's line of travel will be on a bias from right to left. The right hind leg will step over in front of the left hind. It will be the primary load leg because it is directing the horse's mass over to the left. (See Fig. 11.) If the half-pass is ridden on an angle with the shoulders well ahead of the haunches, as many of the old masters demanded, something interesting happens. The body of the horse will be in the way, if you will, of the forward advance of the left hind. Unlike in the renvers where the left inside moves out into space, the left inside leg in the angled half-pass moves more under the body. The result of the half-pass ridden on a bias, well angled into the direction of travel and with good bend in the body, is that both hind limbs can be stressed, albeit in different ways. Nevertheless it makes it unique as a developing exercise.

The modern competitive half-pass is often ridden almost straight – parallel to the wall. This kind of half-pass makes counter changes of hand easier. However, the rider/trainer must always keep in mind that there is an inverse relationship between impulsion – engagement of the hind limbs – and the amount of lateral movement. The more the hind limbs criss-cross sideways, the less power they will have to step under the centre of gravity and propel the horse forward, or upward as in the case of collection. A straight half-pass parallel to the wall can often show more scissoring (crossing over) of the legs, but it will have less engagement and transmit less power. Therefore as a gymnastic exercise which is meant to foster collection, it is inferior.

To summarise – to find the primary load leg in the lateral exercises the rider needs only to determine which hind leg is crossing over in front of the other. That is the leg which is moving closer toward the centre of mass and centre of gravity in order to lift and propel the horse's mass in that line of travel, irrespective of the bend.

If the rider/trainer juxtaposes these exercises in a proper way they can serve as a great tool for suppling with different bends in the body. They also can develop collection by fostering extra work on a particular limb. Perhaps most importantly they can help straighten a horse by developing a more symmetrical loading in both hind legs.

In an issue of the magazine *Parabola* devoted to tradition and transmission, there was a passage quoted from Ibn Khaldun, a fourteenth-century North African historian:

> 'Since it is the nature of tradition to incorporate false statements, we must examine the causes which produce them. They are:
>
> (a) attachments to certain opinions and schools of thought. Now if a man's mind is impartial in receiving tradition, he examines it with all due care so that he can distinguish between true and false; but if he is pervaded by attachment to any particular opinion or sect he immediately accepts any tradition which supports it; and this tendency and attachment clouds his judgment so that he is unable to criticise and scrutinise what he hears, and straightaway accepts [that] which is false and hands it on to others.
>
> (b) over-confidence in the probity of those who hand on the tradition;
>
> (c) ignorance of the real significance of events; for many traditionists, not knowing the significance of what they saw and heard, record events together with their own interpretations or conjectures and so give false information.

(d) belief that one has the truth. This is widespread and comes generally from over-confidence in the narrators of the past;

(e) ignorance of the circumstances surrounding an event induced by ambiguity or embellishment. The narrator hands on the story as he understands it with these misleading and false elements.'[20]

As I have said, in the study of the art of horsemanship we are often bound by a strong oral tradition, and, as Ibn Khaldun has stated, with it by definition there will also be false and misleading messages. In one sense with the continued advance of technology and technique, it is often easier to fix the inaccuracies of science. For the inaccuracies of science, an inquisitive mind will notice, search and find. It is harder to fix the inaccuracies of feeling. Here a rider must close the mind and open the body. So much of riding is the personal way one asks and answers without words. An inaccurate feeling is not one where the student feels something different to that felt by the teacher. All of us are different. So, by definition, we will feel things differently. Inaccuracies come about in how the rider goes about getting his/her feelings. The teacher cultivates the integrity of how you ask and answer. The feeling is between you and your horse.

In that same issue of *Parabola* magazine in the editorial introducing the article, D.M. Dooling says,

'Distortions are in us and all around us and can be as obvious as the folksy tone of modern books on "how to achieve peace of mind" . . . none of us is immune from this kind of distortion; but if we were as honest as we dare and as alert as we might be – as attentive as St Simeon urges – we could save ourselves, and the message, at least from the worst of our own betrayal.'[21]

[89]

If the student and the teacher pursue the art of riding with a flexible mind and with integrity, then, as Dooling suggests, just maybe the message will get through. The interesting part of riding is how you receive and/or deliver the message is one of its biggest messages.

Chapter Seven

Confucius and the Canter Pirouette

'AT WHATEVER PACE [walk, canter, piaffe] the pirouette is executed, the horse slightly bent in the direction in which he is turning, should, remaining on the bit with light contact, turn smoothly round maintaining the exact cadence and sequence of footfalls of that pace. The poll stays the highest point during the entire movement.'

Article 412, Paragraph 4
FEI Rules for Dressage

'The canter is a pace of three-time, where at the canter to

the right for instance the footfalls follow one another as follows: left hind, left diagonal (simultaneously left fore and right hind), right fore, followed by a moment of suspension with all four feet in the air before the next stride begins.'

Article 405, Paragraph 2
FEI Rules for Dressage

'In the canter pirouette the quarters should describe the smallest possible circle, but the horse should not lose the clear three-beat[s] of the canter . . .'

Das Dressur Pferd
Harry Boldt[22]

'In the beginning [of teaching collected canter] many faults may appear: the horse will slacken the movement and drag his hind legs without force; he will become longer in his whole body and his movements will be slovenly; the canter will become four-time instead of three.'

The Complete Training of the Horse and Rider
Alois Podhajsky[15]

'The canter pirouette is developed from the "school canter", which is in fact a four-time canter, though the unassisted human eye is too slow to recognise it as such . . . Nevertheless the pirouette shows more impulsion if the illusion of the three-time canter is preserved.'

A Dressage Judge's Handbook
Brig. Gen. Kurt Albrecht[23]

'In order that the pirouette be judged correct, the horse must go into it in the rhythm of his canter, carrying out the entire pirouette in the same canter, and leaving it also in the same rhythm, which is the great difficulty of this exercise. It loses all its value when it is done with variations of cadence and rhythm by a horse who is unable to do a collected canter in four-time.'

Reflections on Equestrian Art
Nuno Oliveira[2]

The pirouette is to the canter what the piaffe is to the trot. Namely, the ultimate expression of collection in this particular pace. In the same way that I have already stated that I think the piaffe has an obligation to try to remain a two-time movement because its foundation is the trot, I am also from the school that believes the pirouette has an obligation to try to remain a three-time movement because of its foundation in the canter.

Having said that I also know that Brigadier General Albrecht and the late Nuno Oliveira are correct. A pirouette which is executed close to being 'on the spot' or 'the size of a plate behind', will be four-time.

The pirouette has been described as a turn around the inside hind leg, which although acting as the hub must not stick to the ground and pivot. It must be raised up and down on the same spot or move slightly forward in its normal sequence of action. It has also been described as a circle on two tracks in which the radius of the circle is the length of the horse. The pirouette requires the hind legs to scribe a small circle on the ground, often described as the size of a plate. Giving the plate generous dimensions this could be a circle with a circumference of three feet. The front legs stepping sideways scribe another circle, whose circumference is approximately twenty-five feet.

While the horse is scribing these two concentric circles the next requirement of the pirouette is that it maintain the rhythm of canter. So if you enter into the pirouette on a three-beat canter you are supposed to stay in three-beat during the pirouette and as you leave it. In general, a canter will remain three-beat as long as the diagonal pair of legs, which are the second beat, strike the ground simultaneously. If this diagonal pair of legs disassociates, the canter will become four-beat with each leg striking the ground individually in a rotary action – the same way a galloping racehorse moves in a four-beat gait with each leg acting like a spoke of a wheel, transmitting the impulsion forward in even, efficient increments.

In the pirouette, what would make the diagonal pair of legs in the three-beat canter disassociate and create a four-beat canter? One is a clear loss of impulsion and a reduction in the moment of suspension. If the rider enters the pirouette and pulls on the reins he may slow the canter tempo down, which coupled with the difficult turn of the pirouette, will dwindle the suspension phase to almost nothing. This is easy to do if the rider is concentrating too hard on keeping the hind legs 'on the spot', or on a very small circle. In a normal, or even collected, canter the horse floats over considerable ground in the suspension phase. The three beats all help each other to develop the thrust that sends the horse through the air in the moment of suspension. When you ride into the pirouette and practically stop all the forward impetus and limit it to only a few inches of lateral movement, yet you are to keep the same rhythm, the horse would have to literally jump straight up into the air during the moment of suspension. If he didn't, he would not keep the same time in the air as he did in the canter coming up to the pirouette. If the horse changes the time of suspension, he changes the rhythm.

It may be useful to think in musical terms here. Imagine three notes and a pause – corresponding to the three beats and a moment of suspension of the canter. In music the space will be defined and timed. Very often the space becomes as important, or even more important, than the notes. In any case the whole phrase is composed of the four parts. If you play the notes twice in exactly the same way and you shorten the pause once, but not the second time, you have created a slightly different musical phrase. The notes will run together without the space and the overall phrase is shorter, but it will still be recognisable.

This happens in the pirouette all the time because of its great physical demands on the hind legs. It is one thing to shorten the space in the phrase, if you will. However, if in an effort to relieve some of this work, the horse opens up the canter to a rotary form, and gives itself more support by spreading out the limb placement in order to have one leg on the ground at almost all times, then this is tantamount to placing a fourth note in the space. This becomes a very different phrase. When the canter breaks apart in a weak way, avoiding work, it is analogous in its relationship to a true collected canter in the way that the hover trot is related to the passage. Both the broken canter and the hover trot are gaits executed with minimum flexion of the hind legs and therefore with minimum complementary extension.

The second critical matter in what breaks up the three-beat canter during a pirouette will be the number of strides it takes to complete a 360° or full circle revolution. Let's say, for example, a horse takes eight strides to complete the pirouette, making two concentric circles of three feet for the rear legs and twenty-five feet for the front. If the horse is relatively straight in each stride, when the hind legs are moving approximately four and a half inches sideways, the front legs are moving three feet.

[95]

If, for the sake of our argument, a horse cuts the number of strides in half, then when the hind legs move approximately nine inches sideways, the front legs will have to move six feet.

There comes a point when the disparity of these distances puts too much torque on the body. The horse cannot remain relatively straight with the diagonal pair in tact. In an effort to make up the long distance, the front legs will need to help throw the shoulders over. The gait breaks up as each leg leads into the next in a fan-like advance. In the left pirouette, for instance, the right hind starts, and the left hind takes over placed more to the left. The right front is next, even more towards the left, and finally the left front is placed way over to the left. Advancing the canter pirouette in this fan-like four-time rotary manner is much easier on the horse, and can cover much more lateral ground in a single stride. In fact it is the only way a horse can do a pirouette if the rider leaves out too many strides. Instead of pure canter strides with a distinct moment of suspension (enough of a moment of suspension to do a flying change, for example) and great carrying power from the abdominal, hind-end muscles, and the horse's ring of muscle, the horse starts using the shoulders to push the pirouette over and around. This is not collection.

If you agree philosophically that the canter pirouette is a culmination of the canter work, then it seems to me that the emphasis in training has to be more on the canter purity than on the size of the pirouette. This is precisely the essence of of Podhajsky's warning: '. . . a pirouette in which the hind legs turn on the spot, but lose the rhythm of the canter, is a worse fault than one in which the hind legs describe a larger circle but maintain the regular rhythm.'[15]

When Albrecht and Oliveira talk about a four-beat

canter they are not referring to a sluggish, disunited four-beat canter but a school canter which is slightly four beat and has great carrying power behind.

I know it seems like rationalising – one should get off the fence and pick one or the other, three beat or four. Even with great horsemen lining up on either side, it doesn't make it any easier. The study of horsemanship does this to you all the time: presents you with questions that have several answers.

Listen how carefully Seunig writes about the three-beat/four-beat dilemma, how he addresses its existence and then practically apologises for it.

'In the highly developed manège [school] gallop the three-beat gait becomes a four-beat gait because the load rests for an instant only upon the hindquarters, even after the grounding of the inside hind leg. The outside foreleg alights only an instant after the inside hind leg. [The forehand is carried higher.] The difference being hardly perceptible to the observer's senses as in the pirouette. This statement, however, is merely theoretical. In practice, whenever we clearly hear and see the four-beat gait, we also observe that the gallop loses it distinguishing characteristic – the powerful and lively forward engagement of the hindquarters. Its movements lose their fluidity and roundness and become dragging dull, stiff and choppy. . .'[6]

After watching hours of films in slow motion, I agree with Brigadier General Albrecht and Oliveira that it must happen in four time; but, as Oliveira has said, it has to be the right kind of four beat. And when in Albrecht's book it says to try to keep the illusion of three beats, the emphasis shouldn't be on illusion. I don't think he is encouraging any subterfuge. The emphasis is on staying

[97]

close to three-beat. His words are advising us to keep the canter moving!

By now one can see that the canter pirouette is a technical quagmire. If you ride in competitions it becomes practically a moral dilemma. There is only one way you can follow Article 412's requirement of 'maintaining the exact cadence and sequence of footfalls of that pace'. That is, to keep all the canter work in the four-beat school canter so that when you perform the four-beat pirouette you haven't changed the pace. If you do this you violate Article 405 which says 'the canter is a pace of three-time'. If you ride the canter in clear three-time to accommodate Article 405, you will not be able to accommodate Article 412, which insists that you maintain the three-beat rhythm.

It is possible to solve this dilemma?

'The wave-particle duality was (is) one of the thorniest problems in quantum mechanics. Physicists like to have tidy theories which explain everything, and if they are not able to do that they like to have tidy theories about why they can't. The wave-particle duality is not a tidy situation. In fact, its untidiness has forced physicists into a radical new way to perceiving physical reality. . . For most of us life is seldom black and white. The wave-particle duality marked an end to the 'either-or' way of looking at the world. Physicists no longer could accept the proposition that light is either a particle or a wave because they had 'proved' to themselves that it was both – depending on how they looked at it.'[5]

I think a great deal of confusion comes from the limitations of human vision. At regular speed it can be difficult to determine the breakdown of rhythm. In slow-motion films it is easy to see. Very often people who are scoring

[98]

the pirouette have little experience of feeling and training them. Most experienced trainers and riders would not and have not been fooled by the differences of the three-beat canter, the four-beat school or manège canter, and the four-beat broken-down canter. They feel the rhythms and don't really see them. In fact when you ride the pirouette you can never see it. Films are always after the fact, and even if you watch in a mirror part will be blocked from view as you turn. You must learn to feel it.

To this day I still have found no philosophical compromise to the dilemma presented in the literature, the bodies of rules, and the biomechanics of the horse. I have made peace with it in the world of action. To me, the pirouette is not a trick. It is an exercise. Being an exercise it has built into it a relativity, a certain amount of freedom in its form, because the form will be changing as it develops.

The pirouette can be a proof that your horse has mastered bending properly. In order to negotiate those disparate concentric circles the horse's torso has to be flexible. It must be able to move into the tightest of circles without the back stiffening and the horse leaning over on the inside shoulder. The trainer has to remember that the pirouette is still in the family of circles. In that circle the horse, being a quadraped, will leave two lines of tracks – one from the inside front and hind leg, and the other from the outside front and hind leg. Of these two concentric circles the outside one will be larger. One of the earliest requirements of dressage is that the horse's hind feet track along into the same line as the front feet. Although in dressage we say that the horse is then straight, we mean it is bent evenly through the body and it is this bend which allows the horse to stay more perpendicular to the ground, even in tight circles.

A critical fact is that the outside has to be allowed to

[99]

stretch a little in order to cover the longer distance. If the outside rein goes beyond a support or guiding influence to a blocking one (or worse an inversion), the effect is to shorten the outside and either tip the horse onto its inside shoulder, or to force its hindquarters off straightness to the outside. Either of these flaws will be amplified in the pirouette. Once the pirouette is started, the rider should be riding it round with the back, seat and legs which will insure impulsive bounding strides into and through it. He should not be pulling it round with the reins, which will either shift the balance to the forehand or onto a single shoulder.

I have found in training that it is important not to hurry the closing in of the pirouette, but to ride it large in exercises such as renvers to a large passade, or travers to passade to half-pass to counter-canter. After the horse masters steady and equal individual canter strides on two tracks, it will not be difficult to reduce the circles and half circles into rhythmic pirouettes without the danger of spinning or losing the haunches to the outside. I have always preferred these kind of preparatory exercises to spiralling down for that very reason. If the rider is not very experienced it is easy to let the horse fall a little forward so that it starts turning around the shoulder with the hind end escaping to the outside.

When the pirouette is executed in good rhythm it can demonstrate the highest collection in the canter the way the piaffe can demonstrate high collection in the trot. This is a classic principle: that the exercise's real value lies in the gymnasticising or 'dressing' of the horse and not in the display.

Finally I have never given up trying to ride the pirouette in three-beat. To me, it is a reverence for the unattainable goal of pure paces. It is my homage to collection and its gymnastic values and to vigorous impulsion, which must be at the heart of all collection.

Good teachers have always sought to prevent us from having to reinvent the wheel with every new generation. Yet it is this wheel – circle – pirouette – circle metaphor – which is particularly rich and quizzical. We do not have to invent a new movement. We have to execute the one that is here. How we try to do it will reveal everything about our riding. In another sense we do need to reinvent the wheel with every generation. In each relearning more of us get trained, so we learn for ourselves all about the wheel and the circle.

Even if the FEI changed its rules it would not solve the duality presented by the circling pirouette. Certainly it would not stop new dualities from occurring. If the rider/trainer invests all his allegiance to one side when dual things present themselves in riding, which they do all the time, then each negates the other. This kind of causal thinking or mentality can be very limiting in riding as well as in life. Our physicists have already proved that light can be a wave or a particle depending on how you look at it. This is not supposed to be possible. Let me quote from Thomas Cleary:

'In later Chan [Chinese for Zen] schools, it was openly stated that classic texts were meant to be read by putting yourself in everyone's place to get a comprehensive view of subjective and objective relationships . . . In a classical aphorism on education frequently encountered in Chan literature, Confucius said, "If I bring up one corner, and those to whom I am speaking cannot come back with the other three, I don't talk to them any more'.[24]

When Albrecht brings up one corner, the Journeyman rider must bring up the other three. When Oliveira brings up one corner, the Journeyman must bring up the other three. When Podhajsky brings up a different corner, the Journeyman trainer must bring up the other three. When the FEI brings up a corner, the Journeyman must bring up the other three.

If our comprehension of technique approaches that, and if we do not get stuck on one corner, then maybe Confucius will still talk to us.

Chapter Eight

Resistance and Ethics

'WHAT WE DO to animals troubles us – the horror of laboratory experiments, trophy shooting, factory farming – and our loss of contact with them leaves us mysteriously bereaved. If we could re-establish an atmosphere of respect in our relationships simple awe for the complexities of animals' lives, I think we would feel revivified as a species. And we would know more, deeply more, about what we are fighting for when we raise our voices against tyranny of any sort.'

Barry Lopez[25]

I had volunteered myself and one of my horses to be part of some research work being done by a veterinarian from Canada specialising in equine locomotion. This doctor was at the University of Pennsylvania's New Bolton Centre for a short time. A small team was to come over to our farm to film the Grand Prix test and to record heart-rate changes and other data. On the day we chose it was raining very hard but since there were many schedules to consider we decided to stick to the plan and try it in the indoor arena. My horse was fitted with an electrode that could relay heart rates to an expensive monitor set up in the corner. The camera was prepared. The three doctors arranged the equipment with lighted screens. The bright sodium lights of the arena reflected silver off the metal machines. It seemed ironic to be riding some of these ancient exercises under the scrutiny of these high-tech instruments. The horse I was riding was pretty green at this, the most difficult, FEI test, but for the sake of science, we tried. There were some problems with the camera, so the first and second tests weren't recorded. Finally, the machines were all in sync. While I was riding the tests, one of the doctors was monitoring the horse's heart rate. The machine would make a beep that I could hear, and it was in time with my horse's heart beat. Every few seconds, she would announce the computed rate for the film to record. The effect of this was surreal: there, over in the corner, was the electronically beating heart from the horse that was directly under me in all the movements. To hear this beat accelerating and decelerating through the different movements was in itself a revelation. At first I was too engrossed in the novelty to attach much to it. All the doctors were surprised at the horse's fitness from just dressage work. At the end of each test as I halted, the rate was in the lower 100s; by the time I took a couple of steps, and then when I patted the horse the rate would drop into the 60s.

As I finished riding the third test, I made a startling discovery. I had been having difficulty with this horse in the passage. In our practices the resistance in the passage had been increasing. When I pushed the horse on more, the resistance increased. The horse was losing all the suppleness he had in the piaffe, and seemed to be getting increasingly rigid. It was getting to the point where I was re-examining how I was going to proceed. I was feeling that I had to take a new tact in developing this movement. The horse just seemed to be getting too upset and nervous about the whole issue.

As I rode the second test I could hear the heart-rate pulse go up as we did, say, the extended trot, then settle and climb again with the difficult canter work. When I got to the passage, and after repeated attempts, the horse was fuming around in a extravagant effort. I was trying to produce at least some semblance of passage when I heard the heart rate dropping down. I couldn't believe it. I was sure I heard wrong. In the next pieces of passage and in the next test, every time the passage came up, no matter what effort I thought we were putting in, the heart rate went down. I was amazed. This horse was not getting upset from the strenuous passage. He was holding back. Up until that point I was about to back down in the training, or at least try something different. However, it was obvious that I was misreading the horse. At first this bothered me, and on two counts. One, because I felt my judgment was pretty good. My interpretation of the horse's problem was becoming more instinctive and more exact. I seemed to be getting better at isolating the difficulties and selecting exercises which could correct them. However, here I seemed to have really missed.

Second, it bothered me because I felt my partner was somehow disloyal. I was giving my best effort but the horse wasn't. And I didn't even know it. I began seriously thinking about resistances. Is it possible to know all the time what is the real level of resistance? If I can't know, how am I going to proceed? I know very well how some trainers handle problems of resistance...

A rider I know was competing at a famous international dressage show in Europe, and was being coached by a well-known dressage trainer. In the test the horse he rode played up. It didn't really bother that person I know, but it highly embarrassed his well-known trainer in front of his peers. After the show, the horse was taken back to be 'straightened out'. My friend told me that his horse was taken into the woods and beaten with chains.

The rider then had to continue on the competition circuit and in due course the next show came up. I know that every person who ever loved a horse could write a scenario as to how this story should end. However, the reality was different. My friend told me that the horse performed the best test of his life in terms of his score.

There is a nagging fact that in the training of some animals to do certain things brutality will work. Because so many people are riding, and a lot of them are riding in competitions under pressure, you see this kind of training more and more. If you are a trainer of horses you have to address the fact that all over the world horses trained in this manner are receiving praise and recognition in the form of prizes and accolades at riding competitions, and at the highest levels. This is certainly something I have become aware of, and I also realise that it is not new. Historically there are many examples of severe brutality and torture in training horses.

The more I went over the realisation of the heart rate experiment, the more I began to wonder about its significance? What if I was fooled by the horse? What if the horse was cheating? What if I unnecessarily changed the course of training when it really didn't need it? Do you need this kind of absolute mind control in order to proceed? It was not as if I was going to quit training the passage entirely – I was just going to change tracks.

Suppose you have an appointment with someone who is notoriously late. You know almost certainly that if you arrive on time you will waste a half an hour waiting. There is something you could do during that time. Do you still arrive on time? Of course, you must. This imbues your action with an integrity. This integrity is mutually exclusive of any other event. It is not dependent on any other act. It isn't dependent on the outcome.

As a trainer of horses you cannot make a dishonest horse honest. You can make yourself more honest. You can be less deceitful and more open. You become easier to read by virtue of your greater skill. Your actions may become more economical and certainly they become more effective, if for no other reason than because the quality of your communication with the horse is cleaner and less confusing.

You are the one who initiates the training of the horse. You lead, you assume authority. Where does the right to assume authority come from? I would like to quote Vicki Hearne from her book *Adam's Task: Calling Animals by Name*[26] in which she explores, among other training subjects, this one. 'You must realize the ability to exact obedience doesn't give you the right to do so – it is the willingness to obey that confers the right to command.'

The assumption of authority, as Vicki Hearne so ably explains, is nothing unusual. Suppose you see a stranger in danger's way. You shout to him to move; he moves. You have commanded; he has yielded. In the reverse, we yield all the time when it is in our own self-interest. To yield to commands of natural integrity, of course, presupposes the commands have integrity. You take care of your own integrity. You try to arrive on time, all the time. Your intentions are clear. Your commands have integrity. They come out of the same kinds of natural energies that support all of us on the earth – all the other commands.

Who or what does the trainer obey? He or she obeys the code, the way, the life of a trainer. Most of all, the horse. You do not obey the judge, the prize, the trophy. You obey your own integrity. You obey yourself. You have self-respect, and mutual respect. Once you act with integrity, in the issuance of commands, it is almost not your business what the horse does in response. If you are doing your work well, the horse will probably train well. However, if after a long while of your best work, the horse does not respond, there is no more you can do. The horse has decided not to be trained and you may have to let go. If you approach training this way, you will give the horse that ultimate respect. You give it a choice.

If you are a sadistic trainer, who will you obey? Are you going to demand authority over the horse's action? Are you going to demand that you never be fooled? Will you be humiliated if you arrive on time but your appointment doesn't? Are you going to chain the horse into answering your commands?

If you can never be fooled, neither can you be surprised by the mysteries and gifts that animals can bestow upon you.

Too many people assume that they have the right to ride the horse without respect for some proper communication. They have the right to this authority without granting any authority to the horse; without any reverence for the process; without any willingness to be ordered or changed by the horse. If you acknowledge the idea that you go into training the horse with the possibility that you can be changed and ordered by the horse, you have built in a flexibility in your style, a movability in your system, a freedom in your reactions. To further this, you have no choice but to explore and develop your technique in riding. Horses do not speak to people with words. Yet man has been communicating with horses for some six thousand years.[27] The lexicon of his communication with horses is no less than the story of riding. How the trainer handles resistance is directly related to how well he knows the story of riding. If you handle resistance with force, you don't need technique. You need bigger muscles. If you want to handle resistance in other ways, it is going to be directly related to: the level of your skill; the quality of your horsemanship; your knowledge of different options.

In Thomas Cleary's[24] beautiful translation of the two-thousand-year-old Chinese masterpiece of strategy by Sun Tzu, *The Art of War*, he says, 'the master warrior is likewise the one who knows the psychology and mechanics of conflict so intimately that every move of an opponent is seen through at once, and one who is able to act in precise accord with situations, riding on their natural patterns with a minimum of effort.'

Of course, I am not suggesting the trainer is at war with the horse. I am saying that the greater the psychic and physical knowledge of the horse and riding, the better the handling of potential trouble. One has to keep in mind that 'Sun Tzu showed how understanding conflict can lead not only to its resolution, but even to its avoidance altogether.'[24]

This, then, predetermines the masterful rider/trainer to a long and detailed study of technique. In order to advance, (s)he must arrive at the same place that *The Book of Balance and Harmony*, a medieval Taoist text, refers to as: 'A state of deep knowledge'.[24]

'Deep knowledge is to be aware of disturbance before disturbance, to be aware of danger before danger, to be

[109]

aware of destruction before destruction, to be aware of calamity before calamity. Strong action is training the body without being burdened by the body, exercising the mind without being used by the mind, working in the world without being affected by the world, carrying out tasks without being obstructed by tasks.

'By deep knowledge of principle, one can change disturbance into order, change danger into safety, change destruction into survival, change calamity into fortune. By strong action on the Way, one can bring the body to the realm of longevity, bring the mind to the sphere of mystery, bring the world to great peace, and bring tasks to great fulfilment.'

Hasn't that always been the aim of dressage – to bring the horse's body to the realm of longevity, to bring the rider's mind to the sphere of mystery?

I would like to make a strong point that deep knowledge is not easily attainable. Nor should it be taken lightly as some kind of poetic gesture. It is very real and extremely practical. Deep knowledge is not intellectual philosophising. It takes a mastery of a high level of practical psychology and physical development. The modern rider who hires a masseur to prepare the back of his horse may be shirking some of the duties of a rider. This is one of those fundamental tasks that the rider/trainer must know about. Today, people do these kinds of things all the time. This short-circuits the rider's own development, and steps out from under the weight of integrity. It avoids the responsibility to master the lessons, the theory and the material. The Journeyman rider has to try to know these things.

Yet six thousand years of horsemanship can be an imposing study – if not paralysing. By now I have spent thirty years reading and riding. I find myself going back further in time in reading the literature, and I find myself consulting with state of the art scientists on analysis of movement and anatomy. Often the work is redundant. However, every once in a while a sentence will lift me high with some enlightenment. Maybe a riding experience will crystallise a point of technique. To me, this is still exciting. The feeling is revitalising. I love the technical pursuit. Yet I started to realise that the body of knowledge is unknowable. It is too vast and our time on the earth too short. It was hard for me not to be saddened by this realisation. I wasn't going to make it. I saw every day how much I improved from the technical lessons. I wanted to obtain all the information. I wanted to acquire the perfect form. It took a long time before I began to see that wisdom is the knowledge that there is no knowledge. You cannot know a thing completely because it changes all the time. However, you can try to know a thing. The way you try to know something is what life is about. Two thousand years later businessmen read *The Art of War*.[24] Two thousand years later horsemen read Xenophon.[28] Too many of us read them in order to find a way to know or gain something, when really you study something, anything, in order to experience the Way. The relativity of our different skills does not limit any one of us from personal development or enlightenment. When the goal is irrelevant to the glory of the process, the saddness of things unattained is lifted by the rapture of every revelation you do have, every experience you live out.

In the handling of resistance, you don't beat a horse for the things you don't see – the height of the passage that isn't there, which is your own momentary subjective appraisal anyway. The horse may have no idea what it is you are after besides domination. You polish and develop the things that are there. In the case of the horse at the beginning of the chapter, I made headway with the passage when I returned to the piaffe, which was solid. I practised advancing and then collecting the piaffe almost on the spot. The horse learned to stay round with the rein going through the body, instead of hurling himself forward in a hollow passage. He began to extend his piaffe. Riding that develops presupposes that the trainer has a good technical knowledge of how the movements work and which exercises affect which muscles, tendons and ligament groups. The trainer must develop the ability to perceive things other than his own feelings. It is this cultivation of perception that the trainer must seek. An answer to a problem will reveal itself if you know how to look. I mean *how* to look, not where. Even though a book may point you in a direction, eventually the problems are so specific to horse and rider that you fix them while you are riding. What are we talking about is, of course, 'deep knowledge'.

You need to develop 'deep knowledge'. There is a wonderful anecdote illuminating the spirit of this kind of development. It seems the great swordsman Bokuden had three sons all trained in swordsmanship and he wanted to test them.

'He placed a little pillow over the curtain at the entrance to his room, and it was so arranged that a slight touch on the curtain, when it was raised upon entering, would make the pillow fall right on one's head. Bokuden called in the eldest son first. When he approached he noticed the pillow on the curtain, so he took it down, and after entering, he placed it back in the original position. The second son was now called in. He touched the curtain to raise it, and as soon as he saw the pillow coming down, he caught it with his hands and then carefully put it back where it had been. It was the third son's turn to touch the curtain. He came in brusquely, and the pillow fell right

[112]

on his neck. But he cut it in two with his sword even before it came down on the floor.

'Bokuden passed his judgment: "Eldest son, you are well qualified for swordsmanship." So saying, he gave him a sword. To the second son, he said, "Train yourself yet assiduously." But the youngest son, Bokuden most severely reproved, for he was pronounced to be a disgrace to his family.'[1]

It is a similar disgrace for the horseman to routinely use force to overcome resistance and faulty perceptions. The true Journeyman/horseman must also assiduously seek deep knowledge, to avoid battles or force. To understand the Way is more important than the result. When you handle resistance, you handle the tyranny Barry Lopez was talking about in the quote at the beginning of this chapter. If you as a rider/trainer can avoid being an oppressive force from the outside, then you may have a chance to become one with the horse, which may be an overworked phrase, but an underworked reality.

Chapter Nine

The Myths of the Outside Rein

'THE RIDER should not try to support the movement by the aid of the rein; this never leads to true success. Leg and back aids must always be predominant. The horse must learn to move in self-carriage and must only be *guided* and not pulled by the rider.'

Richard L. Watjen[29]

I once witnessed a clinic given by a famous competitive dressage rider, and in the course of three days there were non-stop references to the use of the outside rein. Not one time in three days did I hear any reference to the rider's seat or legs. I was beginning to see that this experience was not unique. Even when a lot of instructors were trying to get their pupils to be lighter with their hands, the instructors' focus of attention never seemed to leave the reins, and so neither did their pupils'.

What this outside rein is all about of course is the turn. If you are riding in a straight line in an open field with no reference to a wall, then theoretically there is no outside rein. To understand the correct and most classical use of the outside rein one must understand the way a dressage horse moves around a circle. This concept is one of the most fundamental and also one of the most pervasive in the whole training of the dressage horse. Before I start analysing the theory of the horse in the turn, and this talk about the outside rein, I would like to make the most important point of this whole topic: **Any and every rein effect must be preceded by a leg or seat effect.** If one imagines a sail boat in a dead calm, you can pull on the sail until you drop but you will not be able to have any steering or guiding effect until some wind force comes from behind to fill the sail with air. This is an obvious and absolute prerequisite. The outside rein functions very much like the sail. It catches power coming from behind, and usually from behind and from the inside. As the wind blows up from behind across the boat. Remember, the wind moves the boat. The sail only helps to guide it. The legs and seat move the horse. The rein only guides it.

All these mechanical analogies have drawbacks. In this one, the hull of the boat is rigid and the horse's body is not. Although some trainers have constantly proposed, and still do, that the horse's body should be as straight as the hull of the ship, this has never been the classical approach. The classical approach has always recognised the bendability of the horse and trained for it in a very

[115]

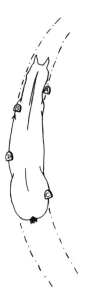

*Fig. 12 When travelling on a circle, the horse follows the arc of circle with an arc
through its body. It should then leave only two imaginary lines of tracks.*

careful way. The trouble with the classical view, though,
is one of very confusing language. One of the most fundamental requirements and descriptions of the dressage
horse is that it is straight when it is evenly bent around a
circle. Yes, it is straight when it is bent. No wonder people get confused about the outside rein! What this means
of course is that when training on a circle the horse follows the approximate arc of the circle with an arc
through its body. It should then leave only two imaginary lines of tracks. The left hind should track on the
same line as the left front, and the right hind tracking
behind the right front (see Fig. 12). The horse then, in
moving around a circle, will leave two lines of tracks or
two concentric circles separated by the distance between
the horse's left and right feet. This leads to some very
interesting developments. The classical horse trainers are
all aware of these.

[116]

The only possible way the horse can track up with both right feet and both left feet in their respective lines is to bend through its body. Now if a horse is travelling on a 10 metre circle and its feet are about 6 inches (or 15 cms) apart, the outside circle scribed on the ground will be approximately 3-6 feet (or 1-2 metres) longer than the inside circle. It is precisely these physical facts which determine the classicists' aids and requirements for negotiating a circle.

One can clearly see that if the outside rein has a retropulsive – or braking – effect, it will restrict the outside stretch and the rider can literally pull the bend out of the horse. There are at least two objective proofs that any horseman can use to see if in fact the horse is too straight on the circle and has lost all bend. One is that the haunches will slip to the outside, so that the tracks of the horse do not line up; the tracks of the hind feet are both outside the tracks of the front feet. Remember, it has always been a key element of dressage training that when the haunches deviate too much laterally, the loading and carrying power are diminished.

The second is that the horse will lean over, to counteract centrifugal force, in the same way that a rigid-framed bicycle has to lean inwards to negotiate a circle and account for centrifugal force. The horse's centre of gravity tips onto the shoulders and the hind legs push instead of carry.

The proper use of the outside rein is to guide the power generated from behind, just as the trimmed sail helps guide the boat. Never does it take an active role and actually bend the neck. This will only succeed in eventually disconnecting the neck from the horse's body and lead to a rubbery neck in front of the withers and a stiff body behind the withers – instead of a flexible body and solidly connected neck, i.e. the horse moving in one piece. The classicist, as Watjen says, can never be a hand rider but must ride the horse predominantly with leg and back aids.

If the rider/trainer always keeps in mind the elementary principles that we train the dressage horse to circle with bend in the body and standing up perpendicular to the ground, and that there must be room for the outside to stretch, then the proper leg aids for circling will also reveal themselves.

So where is the rider's wind power coming from to fill up the outside rein? Obviously, the rider's seat and legs. However, it is easy to see that traditionally the inside leg is stressed. The rider's inside leg can dually act on the horse, not only to move the horse forward by signalling the hind leg on that side to step up more, but also to encourage bend around that leg. So the inside leg generates power into the horse toward the outside rein, which encourages or guides the horse around the curve. Although the rider's outside leg cannot be asleep, it cannot be overactive near the girth or it will push the bend out of the horse and have a discouraging effect on the impulsive travel around the circle. The outside leg needs to be slightly back to catch the haunches if they deviate too much to the outside and to help encourage expanding impulsive steps on the outside of the horse's body. Too much strength and the rider will squash the horse into rigidity between both legs. It is not the easiest thing in the world to have independent leg aids but they are critical to good, free, forward movement. I have seen this many, many times in teaching novice riders. In leg yield, for example, they cannot get the horse to move sideways in spite of what they feel is enormous pressure from their inside leg. When you stand in front of them as they approach you, you can see that every time they use their left leg, for the sake of an argument, to try to move the horse over to the right, their right leg pulses right along with the left. The result is that one signal nullifies the other and the horse continues to go straight in spite of the greatest leg effort from the rider. This is very typical. Even much later in the rider's training, you can see riders playing a kind of ping-pong, chasing the horse's body from one leg to the other, bouncing back and forth without a clear transmission of forward power. To me, it stems from a lack of proper execution of the simplest of figures – the circle.

I have been taught by teachers who were traditional, and those who had Baucherist influences. I was always taught that hand riding was the crudest of riding. It had no place in classical equitation. Even if I did not agree with these teachers philosophically, I would have come to the same conclusion that hand riding was not real equitation, just through the study of technique. One can see in the analysis of the turn alone, how destructive the hands can be. Rough hands will effect every physical and psychological aspect of riding.

Even when pulling on the reins is done under the guise of increasing flexibility, the real effect can be the opposite. While pulling the horse's head from side to side may make the horse respond quicker to the bit and reins, it can disconnect the neck from the body of the horse with the result that the neck is rubbery and the torso is stiff. The horse has been 'broken into two pieces' and it is impossible for the rein then 'to go through the body'. Classical riders have always sought to make the horse flexible in the body.

As I studied some of the old texts and in particular the engravings in the books of Newcastle, Pluvinel, Eisenberg and Guérinière, in spite of many differences and much egotistical posturing, I could not find one illustration with the horse's head and neck bent to the outside.

[119]

Not one. (I found this astounding and yet logical.) Even when the '*pli*', or neck bend, is quite exaggerated, it is still very clear that these riders were all aware of the importance of bend inside. The arc in the horse's body conformed to the arc of the circle they were moving on. This is a passage from one of the Duke of Newcastle's books published in 1667. Preceding this passage he is talking about using his cavesson with a rein tied to it, but listen to the description of how he considers the dressed horse of over three hundred years ago should go around a turn:

> 'For without it [the cavesson rein] no horse can be perfectly dressed, in any kind, to have ply of his neck, and to supple his shoulders, to look into the turn, to have the legs go right, as they ought to in all actions, his body rightly bent to be part of the circle he goes in.'
>
> Duke of Newcastle[30]

One sees a logical progression to Guérinière's invention of the shoulder-in, one of the most masterful inside-bending exercises of all. Guérinière himself pays frequent homage to the preparatory work of the Duke of Newcastle.

> 'We can only seek after the truth in the principle of those who have left us written record of the fruits of their labours and inspirations. Among many authors we have according to the unanimous sentiment of all connoisseurs only two whose works are esteemed, these being M. de la Broue, and the Duke of Newcastle.'
>
> François de la Guérinière[31]

Although Newcastle does not use the term 'shoulder-in', read the following passage and see what exercise comes to mind.

[120]

'Thus the Horse being bias [diagonal] in the inward rein pulled thus [inward] inlarges the horse before, in pulling his inward Foreleg from the outward Foreleg; which puts his inward Hinder-Leg to his outward Hinder-Leg which narrows him behind, makes him bow in the Gambrels [hocks] especially on his outward Hinder-Leg which he rests on and thrusts his inward Hinder-Leg under his belly; which all these things makes him very much upon the Haunches.'

Duke of Newcastle[30]

This is a man who understands collection. So there is this progression to Guérinière and beyond, continuing toward Seeger, Steinbrecht and L'Hotte, up to the modern writer-riders like Watjen and Decarpentry. Make your horse straight. Ride him evenly bent on the circle. The great *pli*, or neck bend inside, was gradually reduced as the riders became more masterful at bending the body vis à vis the shoulder-in, renvers. All this continuing work being based on the inside bend, around a pillar, around the leg. Eventually this bending developed connectedness and straightness.

Today, just as our deep work aims at connecting the horse longitudinally, making the neck and body connected, so proper lateral work has always aimed at this connection of neck, back, and hindquarters. This keeps the integrity of the spine, by enhancing the bend inside and making the outside stretch. Thereby the horse is made supple throughout its length.

So, then, where did so much harsh handwork come from, especially the swinging of the horse's head and neck from side to side that we see everywhere today? I think the greatest single influence was from François Baucher and his disciples, including James Fillis, com-

[121]

pounded by a lot of misinterpretation of his work. When Baucher*, a controversial albeit brilliant rider who performed in circuses in France in the 1800s, came along, he developed a method of training horses. To rid the horse of resistances, he opened the horse's jaws, and bent the horse's jaws and neck, and he bent them a lot – inside and out, up and down, standing still and moving. His work caused a maelstrom of rage, dividing French riders and promoting some Germans to dub Baucher the 'gravedigger of French equitation'. This scenario has many political and social elements in it besides the riding and riding theory. Professor Hilda Nelson has written a wonderful book which illuminates many of these issues, including Baucher's own words. It is critical to understanding the roots of modern riding. James Fillis, who learned from a student of Baucher, went on to develop his own style of neck flexions, specialising in flexions in movement. For me, a lot of Fillis' work can be described by his own words: 'Finally, as the hands are much more effective for guiding than the legs, they should be used in a very light manner.'[32] The photographs that accompany Fillis' book of himself show a rider quite focused on the hands and reins.

Before Baucher you simply do not see neck bending to the outside nor a whole system of bending the neck with the bit and reins. What all this debate turned into was, for one thing, a referendum on hand riding. Although Baucher's work involved many aspects of riding practice and theory, including such things as inventing one-time flying changes, a great portion of his legacy is these neck flexions. It was when these rein pullings and neck bendings occurred in motion, that the real potential for destruction and disconnection came to be. For the horse

---

* For outstanding background information, see Nelson, H., *Baucher, A Man and His Method*, J.A. Allen, London, 1992

to transmit efficient power from the hind legs, a certain amount of rigidity is necessary in the whole torso. If a trainer has a notion to get some false flexibility in the body of a moving horse, it can be at cross-purposes to the biomechanics and cause severe damage to the neck, back and/or rump. It certainly is born out of a misinterpretation of the anatomy of the horse's motion. In all fairness to Baucher, one can't say he advocated what we see today. When one watched someone like Nuno Oliveira ride, who was strongly influenced by Baucher, you never saw pulling on the reins. Whereas if you watch competitive riders trained from the school of Steinbrecht, who warned riders to beware of Baucher and his methods over and over, you can see ferocious rein pulling from side to side.

In terms of this Steinbrecht warning, I once had a conversation with Dr Van Schaik. I made the comment that the current FEI Grand Prix test had some thirty-seven flying changes, not one single complete circular figure except for two canter pirouettes, and was basically connecting all movements by straight lines. I told him I thought Baucher would have loved the test and probably could have designed one very like it. We both agreed that Steinbrecht would probably roll over in his grave at the sight of some the new German riders riding their horses with straight bodies, flexed in the middle of their necks not at the poll, and constantly pulling them from side to side. We both concluded some of these new German riders were perhaps the most Baucherist in the world.[33]

The fact is that bad riding can occur in any school. There is a difficulty today because with fewer and fewer examples of classically dressed horses, plus a general unwillingness to study riding instead of just imitating, many young riders are being inculcated into an acceptance of hand manipulation as a method toward collec-

[123]

tion and lightness, when it is in fact a physical and biological impossibility.

I believe that a lot of trainers who promote neck bending are misapplying Baucher's system. I think they fail to remember that Baucher was often interested in getting his horses off the haunches with the distribution of weight more over all four legs. His system of neck bending with this goal in mind may be argued. However, to claim that rein manipulation can put a horse further on its haunches or collect it, would be quite another matter. Since every rein aid when in motion has the mechanical effect of a hand brake, to a greater or lesser degree, then when a brake is applied to any object in motion, the weight will shift forward. For the horse, the balance goes onto the forehand by definition.

What often happens in excessive neck bending is that the horse comes lighter in the rider's hands but the neck is bent in the middle and the poll is not the highest point. This horse will not be light in the bridle as a result of engagement of the hind legs and a cresting neck promoting bascule and therefore entire lighter forehand. No. The horse will be light in the bridle only by virtue of spitting out the bit and being behind. An objective proof of this kind of riding is that almost invariably these horses will execute poor transitions, and will ride from trick to trick. Horses that are ridden strongly, athletically, without the neck cresting up and out, lose their overall bascule. When the bascule suffers, so does the horse – usually first in the back, and therefore in the transmission of power.

Every way you come to analyse hand riding in daily training and practice, you find trouble. Furthermore it leads riders even further away from the importance of a good seat and dexterity in the legs.

I am certain this is one of the reasons why lungeing the

novice rider has always been a cornerstone of classical equitation. Lungeing forces the rider to make his/her first communications to the horse, and vice versa, through the seat and legs. Since riders are not allowed to hold the reins, they can't rely on the dexterity of their hands. The language becomes clear. It is up to the teachers of riding to insist on the acceptance of the common language of classical riding: the seat, and not the hands. This is not for sentimental nostalgia, but because if one doesn't understand all the reasons why hand riding is crude, including the biomechanical and spiritual, one cannot understand the finer forms of classical equitation.

All the best riders have tried to exalt the horse, to ride it carefully, as a reverent thank you for the gift of travel – real travel towards enlightenment.

However, if you use the horse for travel toward some destination of your ego, you are no better than a bad farmer who has no love for the land, and your horse is nothing but a misused beast of burden. One of those fundamental tasks of the Journeyman is to learn to carry your own burden, and not project it onto other living things.

Chapter Ten

Riding as a Meditation

'"VERY INTERESTING, Dr Jung, very interesting indeed. Now another concept related to motivational development is the process of individuation, which you frequently refer to in your writings. Would you care to comment on this process of psychic development towards a whole, a totality?"

"Well, you know that is something quite simple. Take an acorn, put it in the ground, it grows and becomes an oak. That is man. Man develops from an egg, and grows into the whole man, and that is the law that is in him. . . As each plant, each tree grows from a seed and becomes in the end, say, an oak tree, so man becomes what he is meant to be. At least, he ought to get there. But most get stuck by unfavourable external conditions, by all sorts of hindrances or pathological distortions, wrong education – no end of reasons why one shouldn't get there where one belongs."'

C.G. Jung in an interview with Stephen Blake[34]

In the review of riding literature, the words of the great trainers of the past are heard. Many researchers have claimed to notice a thread among the myriad of inconsistencies and extinct movements, etc. Namely that there are two philosophies in training horses. One philosophy of training bases much of its advice on 'gentleness', 'judicious treatment', and 'naturalness'. This thread is clear in its lineage from the Greek general Xenophon, 400 BC, to Pluvinel, 1555-1620, the Ecuyer to the French King Louis XIII, to Guérinière, 1730, a professional whose reputation is still without match. The second group of trainers of horses had never limited themselves with this attitude. The likes of Grisone, Pignatelli and the Duke of Newcastle never shied away from being extremely rough and severe in the training of their horses. Whether you like it or not both these groups produced highly trained horses. If you read the Duke of Newcastle's work you cannot help but be impressed by his technical prowess. Guérinière himself refers to the Duke of Newcastle's great work many times. If you can get past his ego, his work on freeing the shoulders of the horses, and the correct way to get the horse on its haunches, is amazingly pertinent.

Podhajsky, the late Director of the Spanish Riding School, in his treatise *The Complete Training of Horse and Rider*,[15] states in his own review of the literature and history of the branches of riding that 'as a result of the development of humaneness, the doctrines of the Duke of Newcastle . . . failed to create a durable basis for the art of riding in England . . . The influence built up by Grisone, Pignatelli and their pupils was lost.'

I would love to believe this, but it is impossible. If you go anywhere near a modern dressage show today, right through to the highest levels, you will see and hear many trainers who will not limit themselves to the humane approach. They train and admit that they train in order to win. They demand absolute obedience from the horse and claim they get it or else.

Having studied different writers and trainers for a long time, I now have a different opinion. It is my feeling that is not humaneness versus brutality that divides the two great philosophical schools of riding: it is whether the riding is used for mundane purposes or whether it is realised for its metaphorical meditative properties. This is what separates the lineage of Xenophon, Pluvinel, Guérinière, and those types, from Grisone, Pignatelli, the Duke of Newcastle and their types.

Xenophon was not an animal trainer. Not that there is anything wrong with being an animal trainer. But Xenophon was a philosopher, political man and teacher. He was interested in raising consciousness. It is clear in his writings that he sees horsemanship as another way to do this.

'Anything that is forced can never be beautiful.'[28] This is his language, which is about equestrian art. Webster's Dictionary defines meditation as 'a discourse intended to express its author's reflections or to guide others in contemplation'. Xenophon's book, *The Art of Horsemanship,* is a classical meditation.

Morris Morgan, the English translator of *The Art of Horsemanship*, noted when talking about Xenophon's equestrian writings: 'One likes to believe the both (books) were designed by the old soldier to serve for the guidance of his sons.' Xenophon was well aware that work with horses has metaphorical properties, and meditative value. His writings clearly reflect this as opposed to being only a treatise on animal behaviour or horse training.

If you read Pluvinel's writings you will see he is partially obsessed with the consciousness-raising of France's youth at a time when they were killing each other in senseless duels.[35]

His love of and skill in riding was a way to pursue personal development. There is no question as to riding's use as a meditative and physical exercise. 'Thus your majesty can see quite clearly how useful this beautiful exercise is to the mind, since it instructs and accustoms it to perform with clarity and order all these functions amid noise, worry, agitation, and . . . fear. . .'[35]

In the beginning of the first chapter of the second section of Guérinière's book, *Ecole de Cavalerie*,[31] he talks about the qualities necessary to become a horseman and why there are so few real horsemen.

'Practice without true principles is nothing other than routine, the fruit of which is an execution strained and unsure, a false diamond which dazzles semi-connoisseurs often more impressed by the fineness of the horse than by the merit of horseman . . . This scarcity of principles renders pupils unable to distinguish short-comings from perfection. They have no other recourse but imitation.'

Now the eminent psychologist C.G. Jung:

'Human beings have one faculty which, though it is of

[129]

the greatest utility for collective purposes, is most perni-
cious for individuation, and that is the faculty of imitation . . . as a rule these specious attempts at individual dif-
ferentiation stiffen into a pose, and the imitator remains
at the same level as he always was, only several degrees
more sterile than before. To find out what is truly individual to ourselves, profound reflection in needed, and
suddenly we realise how uncommonly difficult the discovery of individuality is . . . You cannot imagine how
one-sided people are nowadays. And so it needs no end
of work to get people rounded out, or mentally more
developed, more conscious.'[34]

This psychological meditational approach is not specific
to equestrian art at all. In the Orient (even during this
same time) practitioners of the martial arts were understanding and espousing the mental – psychical – aspect of
their art. They were exploring the metaphorical qualities
of their disciplines and their value as meditations capable
of developing self-awareness, self-enlightenment and
natural understanding.

In Hans Joachin Stein's book about Kyudo, the *Art of
Zen Archery*, he (a German studying in the Orient) talks
about meditation:

'Meditation, in whatever form, with or without a bow, *as
contemplation it has always been known to us*. If such
meditation is practised for its own sake without any
intentionally determined aim, our belief in the existence
of an individual (I) confronted by the universe will gradually fall away as we return to our Self. That will happen
as gently and unresistingly as a leaf detaches itself from a
branch in autumn. We shake off the chains of our I with
its desires and cravings. The opposites return to the unity
of the whole. The meditator experiences a deep inner

calm which makes him immune to the externalities of his every day life – and yet he will not resist them.'[36]

Pluvinel again: 'Riding instructs and accustoms the mind to perform with clarity and order all these functions amid noise, worry, agitation and . . . fear. . .'

Modern Kendo is the way of the sword or swordmanship. A dull bamboo sword is conventionally used in practice. This sword is a vehicle but it is not capable of cutting through an opponent. Its real use is to cut through one's own ego. The study of sword fighting is metaphorical, meditative, a physical and mental developing exercise to get at life itself. In horsemanship the vehicle of enlightenment is the horse, and the horse is nature itself. This is one of the reasons for the rich mythology involving horses and men. Since the horse is nature itself, the lessons are incredibly profound. The moment the horseman/rider succumbs to the lessons of the horse, they have transcended the duality of man and nature, man against nature. For modern western philosophy, this can be a great jump. However, if it happens, the I-ego dissolves, and the rider sees right into nature, his own and the horse's which are, of course, from the same source.

Anila Jaffe wrote a book on the life and work of C.G. Jung. She told how the great psychologist Jung came upon the ancient Chinese meditational text, *The Secret of the Golden Flower*, how profoundly it pressed him into some of his greatest insights:

'Above all there was an affinity between the goals to be reached: the production of the diamond body through meditation was a symbol for the shifting of the psychic centre from the ego to a transpersonal, spiritual authority. The meditative process thus involved a psychic trans-

[131]

formation which Jung had recognised and experienced as the goal of individuation, the recession of the ego in favour of the totality of the self.'[37]

There is another famous quote of Jung's which goes, 'the man who must win at something has not yet arrived'. Arrived where? Arrived at the totality of the self, the development of the self. The Journeyman rider knows this place well. To get stuck in this world of winning at something means the totality of the self cannot be reached because the ego won't recede. The ego stops the rider's development on all levels and leaves him an imitator, not just on a personal level but on a technical level also. So Jung's oak tree is stunted.

Returning to riding's two great philosophies, we have on one hand an animal behaviour training system. Reward the horse for the desired response, punish him for the undesired response. Give the horse a carrot. Reward the rider for the desired response with a prize. These are externally applied systems of gratification. For the rider it only works for a rider 'who has not yet arrived', who has stopped on the road to his own enlightenment, his own individuation. The ego reigns in these places. It will not recede. The rider can't further develop and must be vulnerable to manipulation from the outside. The whole process gets arrested on a certain plane.

Riding's second philosophy is that the act and art of riding is in itself the reward, the path to enlightenment, education, self-development. The gratification is determined internally, as each individual reaches his or her own very unique potential. As long as the process is in motion, it has to be right.

I don't think that experienced horsemen practising the humane school of riding necessarily believe that this is a superior animal-training system. In some cases brutality is an easier route when you are trying to eliminate or develop certain behaviour – manipulate horses, or people for that matter. However, if you are using riding as a meditation, a way to explore yourself and nature, a way to get through, as Jung says, the 'pathological distortions, wrong education – no end of reasons why one shouldn't get there where one belongs'.[34]

Expedience, then, is not the only criteria. There are some obvious observations. The horse is nature. You are Nature. Horse and man are in the same world, with a commonality. Brutality to nature is brutality to yourself. Brutality toward the horse is doubly destructive; destructive to the horse, as well as destructive to the person riding the horse. The doctrine of humaneness comes from this meditation and not from a search for the most cost-effective way to get the horse to do what the trainer/rider wants. (It is almost as though one says it is not really that I care how the horse feels after I brutalise it, it is how I will feel after I brutalise it.)

All along in my Journeyman stage I thought a technical thread would appear if I studied the lineages and exercises hard enough. In my search for the purest line of riding technique, the best exercises, the only airs, I talked to and read classical trainers and circus trainers and competitive trainers, past and present. I couldn't find clear threads. When I studied movements like ballotade, capriole, courbette, croupade, demi-volte, volte, falcade, ferme à ferme, mesair, pessade, passage, passade, levade, pirouette, shoulder-in, terre à terre, un pas un saut, Spanish walk, Spanish trot, and so on and on, I couldn't find real reasons for certain ones' extinctions and others' popularity. It became apparent that a lot of technique was accepted or rejected not as much on physical anatomical, or scientific horse-related reasons as much as it was accepted because of the virtuosity and charisma of certain

[133]

trainers. The more I studied the movements through history, the more I saw how they have changed. It is impossible to base the idea of riding classically on the performance of certain movements alone. Saying this or that exercise is classical can become increasingly cloudy the deeper you research them. My continuous study of technique kept showing me that the movements themselves were not the glue of classical riding.

In all my searchings I did not find the thread of Xenophon, Pluvinel on Guérinière to be a technical one. I did find a thread, though, and it was a metaphysical one. It was aesthetic. It was artistic. I was beginning to see that even if and when riding was dazzling in technical bravura, unless it made the step from mundane to meditation, it could not be art. No matter how great the technique, the rider could get arrested from arriving. I think it can be said that both philosophies of training produced well-trained horses, but only one also produced well-trained men.

Being arrested in the technical plane in the Journeyman phase can be described as being stuck in a certain plane of psychological development. Namely, stuck in the world of the ego. Both technical and psychological growth can falter as the human organism searches for a totality that it knows deep inside is out there. Since each of our potentials is unique, they really can't be compared. Each must follow the plan mapped out for that person in a sense at birth. The oak must become the oak, the spruce, the spruce, etc.

The glue of classical riding is the aesthetic, with its strong and profound mythological connections, which are vast. There is Pegasus, and Quixote's horse. When the knights Gawain and Galahad search for the Holy Grail it is on the backs of horses. 'When Mohammed was flown to heaven it was on the back of a horse. At the end of time the Messiah and Vishnu are supposed to descend from the clouds on horses. It was a dragon horse from heaven that revealed the forces of the Universe, the Yin and the Yang, to the Yellow Emperor of China.'[38] It goes on and on. The Horse, the superior mover, carries man.

Towards the end of my time as a Journeyman, I had a strong and vivid dream-like image appear. I was riding fast across a wide, big, arid plane. The ground was dusty and dry, the vegetation browned and tanned from a long season of heat. Waves radiated off the hot earth. I could see all the way to the blue sky horizon. Far in the distance in the direction I was going I could see another/rider standing still on a small rise. His image shimmered in the heat waves but I could see he was on a white Spanish horse. The only movement I could detect was the occasionally swish of the horse's wide tail. As I approached closer, my own horse leaving a trail of powdery dust, I could see that the rider was an old man. He seemed thin, almost frail, on top of the beautiful horse, but he looked comfortable, the way old horsemen sit on horses – better than they do on chairs. I kept approaching. He seemed to be waiting. I was too far away to make out any of his features but I was aware of his eyes. Somehow I could sense his light-coloured, squinting eyes set in his wrinkled face. I knew they were staring at me. They were not menacing eyes. They were kind eyes, and somehow I felt they were approving, patient eyes, accepting eyes. I kept up the pace. The waves seemed to settle his image, which became clearer. But he remained motionless. The closer I got, the older he seemed to look, and yet there was something familiar in his form. I got even closer, my horse still in strong motion. Then, with enough shock to stop my horse in full arrest, I recognised the old man.

It was me.

I was looking at myself in both directions of time. Seeing myself as an old man. In the same moment I could feel one part of myself flying toward the end of my own life, and the other part quietly waiting for the younger part. The young man rides to the old man. The old man waits to accept the young man. I saw the struggle of the Journeyman in this image: the movement toward the final stages, and the acceptance of growth; the inevitability of movement in time and the advance of age; the necessity to address it, to believe it, and to allow maturation and growth toward it. I saw the horse, the great carrier, the mythological horse that carried men through the dark forests of complacency, across the desert of conformity and imitation. The horse, always man's fearless companion, his most trusting ally, could carry him through any danger, through all those distortions that keep a man from being where he should be. I saw that the beautiful horse was, in the end, always ready to carry me toward my own real self. Somehow the horse knows that you are out there waiting for yourself. The horse will help the man. I began to feel that in the end this is the only job worthy of the horse's effort: not to serve a man's childish egocentric impulses and insecure desires – these jobs demean the horse and the lessons of the mythology. The horse, it seems, has always been there to help carry the man to his own real self, if the rider wants that challenge.

'There is a wonderful image in King Arthur where the knights of the Round Table are about to enter the search for the Grail in the Dark Forest, and the narrator says, "They thought it would be a disgrace to go forth in a group. So each entered the forest at a separate point of his choice." You've interpreted that to express the Western emphasis upon the unique phenomenon of a single human life – the individual confronting darkness.'

Bill Moyers[39]

[136]

Joseph Campbell, the great teacher and mythologist, answers the journalist Moyers:

> 'What struck me when I read that in the thirteenth century Queste del Saint Graal, was that it epitomizes an especially Western spiritual aim and ideal, which is, of living the life that is potential in you, and was never in anyone else as a possibility.
>
> 'This, I believe, is the great Western truth: That each of us is a completely unique creature, and that, if we are ever to give any gift to the world, it will have to come out of our own experience and fulfillment of our own potentialities, not someone else's.'
>
> Joseph Campbell[39]

Epilogue

THE SCIENTIST HILDEBRAND defines four hundred different strides and concludes that there is no such thing as stride. The scientist Wentick studies the physiology of muscle movement only partially in a single leg and its complexity can bring smoke out of a computer. Dr Leach tell us there is a whole continuum of limb patterns. When you study the historical literature, it is filled with riding movements and gaits that are extinct. The most prestigious classical riding school in the world practises some movements that are younger than some chairs in the building.

Once you begin to study the movement of the horse, and once you begin to study the historical literature, you learn to be careful about what or whom you call 'classical'.

My own study of riding forced me over and over out of my presumptions, biases and prejudices. One must learn to handle these inevitable dualisms in riding. As they say in Zen, you learn to take the middle path. In spite of the paradoxes and apparent confusion about classical riding, it actually has become more solid to me over the years of training horses. For the horse and its dressage movements, I have come, like others before me, to put the emphasis on what comes naturally to the horse. In some thirty years of observing horses, I have never seen an untrained horse canter backwards or on three legs. I have seen untrained horses do flying changes and even multiple flying changes. So I consider flying changes to be a natural movement for the horse and therefore suitable for enhancement through (dressage) training. I have never seen an untrained horse do Spanish walk. I have seen countless untrained horses passage in excitement when a new horse enters a pasture. So, to me, the passage is natural for the horse and can be classically adapted. I have a three-year-old horse in my barn at the moment, that is barely broken. She will break into an expressive piaffe in her stall if a lawn-mower comes too close to her window. I have seen horses extend and collect all their paces. I have seen pirouettes and plenty of leaps and levades as young horses play.

This naturalness then has become my criteria for which movements are classical. Even though classical has come to mean many things to many people, I have come to agree with those writers and riders who insist on keeping the integrity of what is natural for the horse. Classical riding is an artistic homage to nature

What about for the human? What is the quintessence of the classical rider? Certainly the Journeyman phase is one thick with technique, and yet, I myself hit a certain wall, focusing only on the technical plane. I knew any real advancement was going to have to come on a different plane, a metaphysical, spiritual, psychological plane. The study of technique is arduous. It is painful. You will need discipline. Here, many riders go astray. They use the discipline as punishment for their apparent failures in achievement the same way they use a prize for reward. 'I only got the second prize. I have to work harder, drive myself and my horse harder,'; 'My practice isn't good enough yet.' Pain becomes the big feeling as the work crackles with ambition. Ironically this is the way of the loser. Failure is built in when everything must be measured by those riders. Everyone must be compared and ranked. Their minds are engrossed in calibration. It becomes the way of the unbalanced mind. This trouble is very serious because it is the way of death. Horses today are dying and people are dying inside and out as a result of unbridled ambition and relentless egos. All this pain and anger. All this mentality. What does this mind fear? Rejection? What does this mind want? Acceptance, recognition, respect? All this misused discipline and torture to get something from the mind. What this mind really wants is something the mind can't give. This mind really wants something from the heart. Something like love. But the heart can't be tricked out of it. The heart can only give to another heart.

So every rider will come to a fork in his or her path. Choosing the path of the winner, will make you the loser. Yet there is another way. Not the Way of Death, but the Way of Life. If you choose this path, then you will need all the discipline you can possibly come by. Childish tantrums won't help here at all. It is the most difficult path. All the work of the Journeyman will be necessary if you want to come out alive, and this is no metaphor. I mean literally alive. Many people never find themselves. They become a construct of other people's opinions and ideas about them. This becomes their guiding light. What was unique in them has disappeared. They become imposters. 'I am what my father always wanted me to be/what my mother expected,'etc. 'There was not time to find the original me, and that is OK because maybe I wouldn't like me.'

No one will really be able to help you on your Journey. Sometimes because they don't want to. Even the people closest to you may try to talk you out of it; maybe even impede you because of their own fears of change, theirs or yours. Yet the Way of Life is the Way of Changes. Sometime even people who love you still can't help just because they are in a different place. We are all so different that it would be presumptions to try to stand in the way of someone's destiny for good or bad reasons.

One has to prove oneself in the technical and theoretical areas. Learning to ride is not learning to compete. If you think this is so, you may have to go to a big show, ride and then leave before the prizes are given out or before the assessments of others are voiced. Especially if you've never done it. Go home. Alone. See what you feel like. See if you know what happened. See if you know if it was good enough. See if you can sustain yourself. If you go to watch the show, you should do the same. Leave early and see if you know for yourself what happened. The Journeyman cannot project his own missing face onto the spirit of the horse. That was something certainly I was unwilling to do any more. The horse could carry me but as my respect for the horse grew and grew, I knew it was not put on the earth to carry my goals and ambitions, all the weaknesses, as Jung might say, that keep one from becoming a complete man or woman. No one has the right to project one's imperfect view or analysis of

[141]

what life should be onto another living thing in the world.

It is in the proving of oneself that this second path comes about. So you learn all you can. All the technique to keep you calm and strong. All the discipline will be necessary now so you won't fall apart when you let yourself get out of control. When you begin the hardest phase of riding. When you run with the highest technique. When you fall in love with riding.

References

1. SUZUKI, DAISETZ, T. *Zen and Japanese Culture*, Princeton University Press, Princeton, New Jersey, 1970.
2. OLIVEIRA, NUNO, *Reflections on Equestrian Art*, J.A. Allen, London, 1976.
3. NEWCASTLE, DUKE OF, *A General System of Horsemanship*, 1627.
4. PRATT, G.W. JNR, Remarks on Gait Analysis, Dept of Electrical Engineering and Computer Science, MIT, Cambridge, Mass. and Tufts University School of Veterinary Medicine, Boston. Mass.
5. ZUKAV, G., *The Dancing Wu Li Masters*, Bantam Book, New York, 1980.
6. SEUNIG, WALDEMAR, *Horsemanship*, Doubleday and Company Inc., New York, 1956.
7. DREVEMO, S., FREDRICKSON, I., DALIN, G., and HJERTEN, G. (1980b), Equine Locomotion. 1. 'The analysis of coordination between limbs of trotting Standardbreds,' *Equine Vet. Jnl*, 12, 66-70.
8. ROONEY, J.R., *Biomechanics of Lameness in Horses*, William and Wilkens, Baltimore, 1969.
9. PRATT, G.W. JNR, and O'CONNOR, J.T. JNR, (1976), 'Force plate studies of equine biomechanics,' *Am Jnl Vet. Res.*, 37, 1251-1255.
10. DREVEMO, S., FREDRICKSON, I., DALIN, G., and HJERTEN, G. (1980a), Equine Locomotion. 1. 'The analysis of linear and temporal stride characteristics of trotting Standardbreds', *Equine Vet. Jnl*, 12, 60-65.
11. SCHRYVER, H.F., BARTEL, D.L, LANGRANA, N., and LOWE, J.E. (1978), 'Locomo

tion in the horse: kinematics and external and internal forces in the normal equine digit in the walk and trot,' *Am. Jnl Vet. Res.*, 38, 1728-1733.

12. KINGSBURY, H.B., QUADDUS, M.A., ROONEY, J.R., and GEARY, H.E. (1978), 'A laboratory system for production of flexion rates and forces in the forelimb of the horse', *Am. Jnl. Vet. Res.*, 39, 365-369.

13. GOODY, PETER, *Horse Anatomy, A Pictorial Approach to Equine Structure*, J.A. Allen, London, 1976.

14. DECARPENTRY, GENERAL, *Academic Equitation*, translated by N. Bartle, J.A. Allen, London, 1971.

15. PODHAJSKY, ALOIS, *The Complete Training of Horse and Rider*, Doubleday and Company Inc., New York, and Harrap, London, 1967.

16. Interview with Reiner Klimke by Christian Thiess, *Dressage & CT Magazine*, February, 1994.

17. BENNET, DEB. PhD, *Principles of Conformation Analysis*, Vol 1, Fleet Street Publishing Corporation, Gaithersburg, MD, 1990.

18. TOWNSEND, H.G.G., LEACH, D.H., FRETZ. P.B., 'Kinematics of the equine thoracolumbar spine', *Equine Vet. Jnl*, (1983), 15, (2), 117-122.

19. PODHAJSKY, ALOIS, *The Riding Teacher*, Doubleday and Company Inc., New York, and Harrap, London, 1973.

20. IBN KHALDUN, *Parabola*, Vol. XIV, No. 2, May, 1969.

21. DOOLING, D.M., *Parabola*, Vol. XIV, No. 2, May, 1989.

22. BOLDT, H., *Das Dressur Pferd*, Edition Haberbeck,Germany, 1978.

23. ALBRECHT, K., *A Dressage Judge's Handbook*, J.A. Allen, London, 1978.

24. TZU, SUN, *The Art of War*, translated by Thomas Cleary, Shambhala, Boston and London, 1988.

25. LOPEZ, B., 'Renegotiating contracts', *Parabola*, Vol. VIII, No. 2, May, 1983.

26. HEARNE, V., *Adam's Task: Calling the Animals by Name*, Vintage Books, Random House, New York, 1986.

27. ANTHONY, D., TELEGIN, D., BROWN, D., 'The origin of horseback riding', *Scientific American*, December, 1991, pp 94-98.

28. XENOPHON, *The Art of Horsemanship*, J.A. Allen, London, 1962.

29. WATJEN, R., *Dressage Riding*, J.A. Allen, London, 1958.

30. NEWCASTLE, DUKE OF, *A new method and extraordinary invention to Dress Horses and work them according to Nature: as also to perfect Nature by the Subtilty of Art which was never found out, by the Thrice Noble High and puissant Prince, William Cavendish, 1667.*

31. GUÉRINIERE, F., *Ecole de Cavalerie*, 1751.

32. FILLIS, J., *Breaking and Riding*, J.A. Allen, London, 1986.

33. Video tape: 'Warming up in Aachen', Dressage at Aachen, 1991, Cloverlea Dressage Videotapes, Columbia, Connecticut, 16237.

34. MCGUIRE, W. and HULL, R.F.C. (editors), *C.G. Jung Speaking: Interviews and Encounters*, Bollingen Series XCVII, Princeton University Press, 1977, pp 324, 276, 256.

35. PLUVINEL, ANTOINE, *Le Maneige Royal*, J.A. Allen, London, 1989.

36. STEIN, H.J., *Kyudo: The Art of Zen Archery*, Element Books, Dorset, 1988.

37. JAFFE, A., *From the Life and Work of C.G. Jung*, Diamon Verlag, Einsieden, Switzerland, 1989.

38. VAN BOREN, A., *Parabola*, Vol. VIII, No. 2, May, 1983.

39. MOYERS, BILL, Interview with Joseph Campbell, *The Power of Myth*, Doubleday and Company Inc., New York, 1988.